THE FANTASY COOKBOOK

From a time beyond recall,
From a land that's ever more,
Come, we bid you see
A land of living fantasy.
This is the land of Zir,
A world of great beliefs.
This is the land of life,
A place of magic feasts.

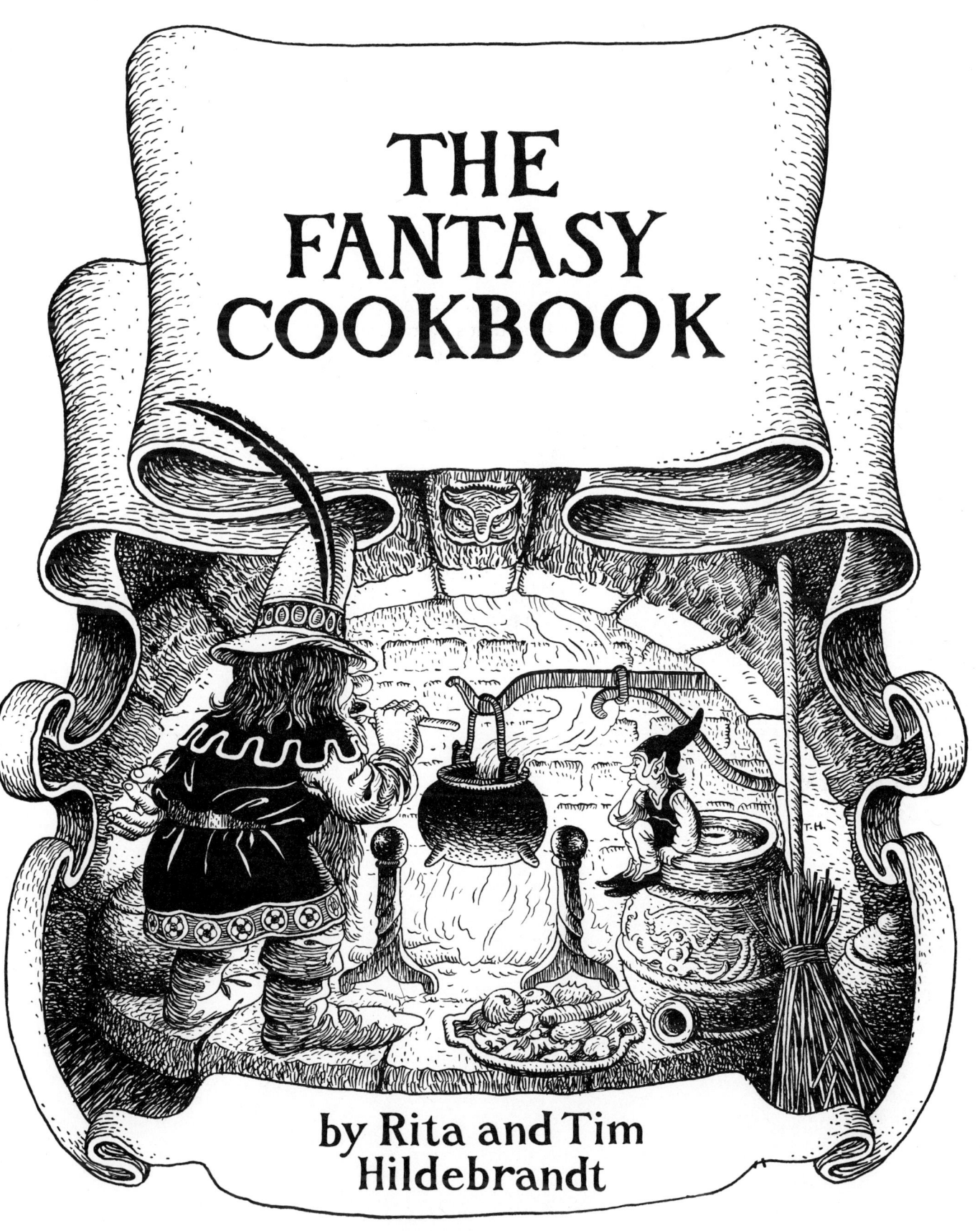

THE FANTASY COOKBOOK

by Rita and Tim Hildebrandt

The Bobbs-Merrill Company, Inc.
Indianapolis/New York

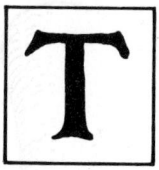his book is dedicated to my parents for they always provided me the important time and freedom to enter the world of fantasy and to my husband, Tim, and my son, Charles George, with whom I have shared that world.

Special thanks to my assistant, Charlotte Wieland, whose creative input and devotion to this book made the project so much fun.

A note of gratitude to my grandmother, Anita Huron Herrera, my mother-in-law, Germaine Hildebrandt, and Mary Ann Glynn for their culinary help.

Thanks to Lorraine Lenches for her typing, and to my editors, Barbara Lagowski and Barbara Reiss, for their imaginative input and enthusiastic support throughout this project.

Models:

William J. Lenches
Abigail Wieland
Terrence Glynn
John Archibald
Anthony J. Oestreicher
Lisa Lenches
Leslie Lenches
Sue Oster

Ken Walker
Frank Balsamo
Gregory Ramoundos
Kathi Vent
Brigid Glynn
Kathy Glynn
Christain Moore
Charles George Hildebrandt

Donna Jayne Trucksess
Sam Golub
William J. Lenches, Jr.
Tracy Fagan
Joe Kaufmann Jr.
Lucy
Godfrey

Copyright © 1983 by Rita Hildebrandt
Illustrations Copyright © 1983 by Tim Hildebrandt
All rights reserved.
No part of this publication may be reproduced, stored in a retrieval system or transmitted in any form or by any means, mechanical, electronic, photocopying, recording, or otherwise without the prior written permission of the publisher. For information, address
The Bobbs-Merrill Co., Inc., 630 Third Ave., New York, N.Y. 10017

Published by The Bobbs-Merrill Co., Inc.
Indianapolis/New York
Manufactured in the United States of America
First Printing
Designed by Delgado Design Associates

Library of Congress Cataloging in Publication Data

Hildebrandt, Rita.
    The Rita and Tim Hildebrandt fantasy cookbook.

    Includes index.
    I. Hildebrandt, Tim. II. Title.
TX652.H54   1983   641.5   82-17798
ISBN 0-672-52703-0

INTRODUCTION   vii

THE DWARFS   1

THE AMAZONS   31

ALZAR THE WIZARD   63

THE ELVES   91

THE TROLLS   119

THE FAIRIES   137

THE MERPEOPLE   159

SPECIAL INGREDIENTS   184

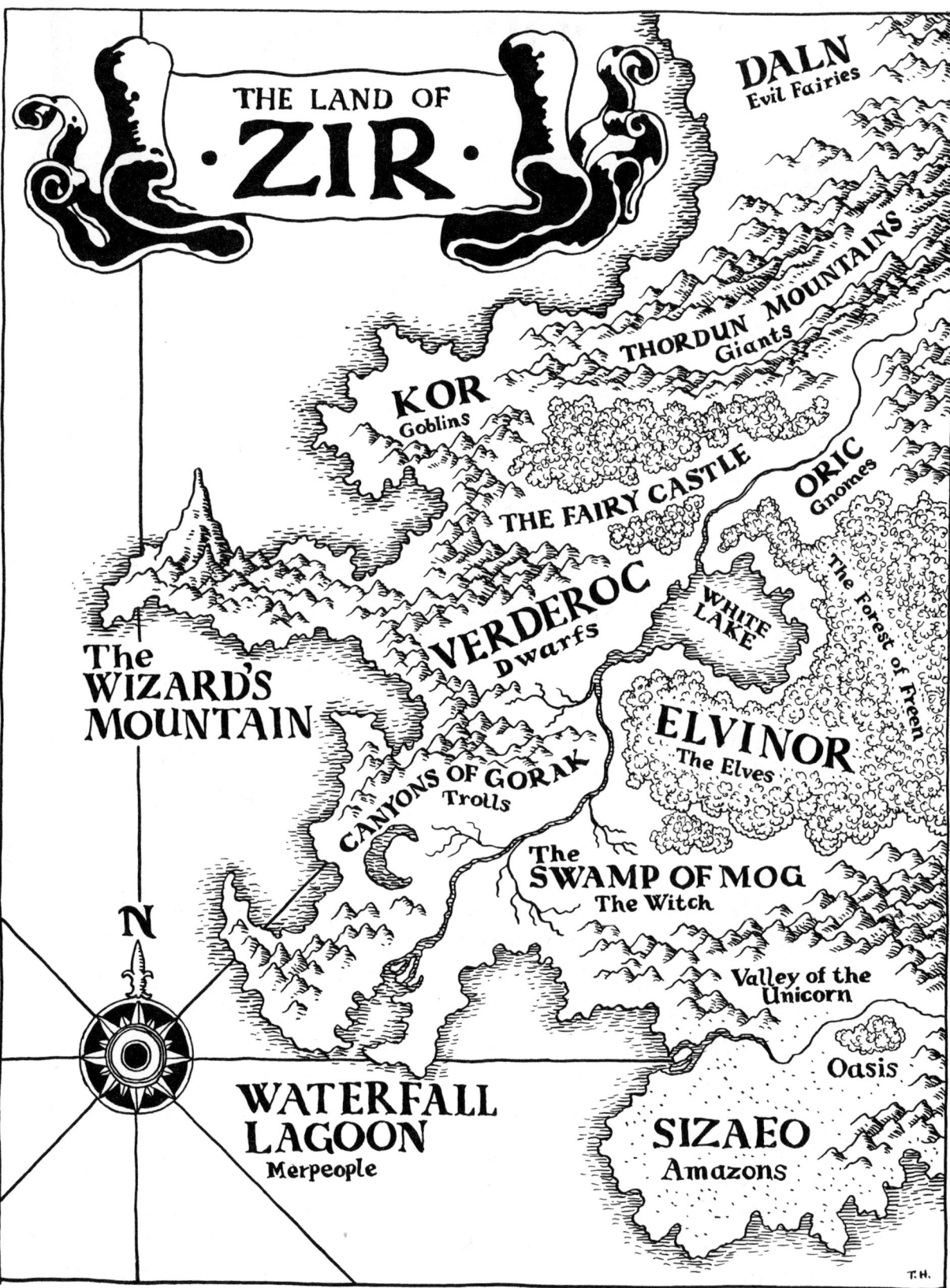

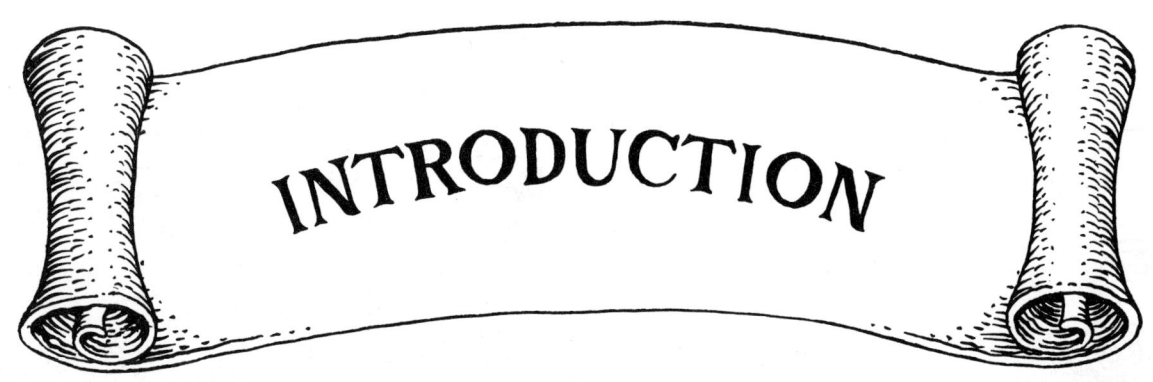

INTRODUCTION

From the time I took my first cake out of the oven at age nine till now, many cakes later, my desire to write a cookbook surfaced consistently in conversations or daydreams. Busy with designing costumes, teaching, and my family, I kept my idea on the back burner until the snow-laden February morning that changed the course of my life.

Up in the third-floor tower room of our Victorian home, absorbed in my collection of old books, I was surrounded by the comfortable clutter of bottles filled with buttons, laces, and other sewing supplies. Facing a work table covered with patterns and pieces of fabric, I was startled by the insistent ring of the doorbell. I ran downstairs, reaching the second-floor landing before it occurred to me that the old doorbell had been broken since the day we bought the house. How could it now be ringing?

I swung open the front door and found a young man about four feet tall standing on the snowy porch. Under his arm he carried a large red book fastened shut with a silver and gold clasp. "May I come in?" he asked.

To my astonishment I answered, "Of course, don't stand out there in the cold!"

He stepped inside and handed me the book. I glanced at it briefly, and when I looked up he was gone.

It was the gift of a lifetime, a magic book, written in an unearthly language that, somehow, I instantly understood. The book was a history of the continent of Zir, a magical chronicle nearly as alive as the people whose lives it described. The figures in the illustrations moved, music played, and food could actually be smelled and tasted simply by looking at the pictures.

Each Ziran society has its own form of cooking and uses specific ingredients and techniques rooted in ancestry and social structure. For example, the regal, black Amazon women do not cook at all like the slow-witted, clumsy trolls, and the robust cooking of the gregarious dwarfs differs greatly from the delicate cuisine favored by the fairies. (Though there are several types of fairies, the cooking of all the fairy groups is basically the same.)

At first my family and I used the book for our own pleasure. Through it we came to know the people of Zir and learned their ways. I began duplicating the clothes of each society while my husband studied the architecture. Soon, however, the delightful recipes drew my fascination, and I eagerly began trying to re-create the dishes I found in the book. As my file of recipes grew, I began to invite friends over for a "dwarf dinner" or a "fairy tea," sometimes complete with costumes!

I spoke openly to friends and relatives about our wonderful gift. There were those, of course, who thought the book's magic was my own wishful thinking, but I found some who listened and some who even came to believe.

Somewhere in the middle of it all I realized that this was the cookbook I always wanted and waited so long to write. It is my hope that you will enjoy the cuisines special to each society, shaped by their various climates, social order and magical development. You will not become a dwarf if you drink their mead, nor will you turn into a troll by eating their stews; whether or not you will gain any magical powers, I cannot say. I can only promise that the good taste of these fine dishes will bring pleasure to you, your family, and friends.

The word *dwarf* means "united" in an ancient language. Long ago two tribes joined forces for their mutual survival and created the dwarf society as it is known today. It is a unique society that melds the magical talents of miners with the diverse skills of farmers to produce a balanced way of life. The dwarfs tend their fields during the growing season, then work in the mines during the winter months when their fields lie fallow. They are loosely governed by a council of chieftains and a titular king. They live in a fertile area of Zir called Verderoc.

Family members work together closely, sharing all the household chores. It is not uncommon for husband and wife to work in the fields side by side or to build a house together. The dwarfs believe that when more than one dwarf undertakes a job, it becomes a party — and then nothing is too difficult. All this sharing of work creates time for each individual to pursue personal interests. Traditionally, mining is the only task not done by children or womenfolk.

Dwarfs are depicted in tales as sensitive, gregarious hoarders of gold who are vengeful toward those who cross them. This picture is not altogether true, however. In fact, they can be very generous with gifts and favors.

Many activities occupy a dwarf's time, but food and eating dominate his life. If the truth be known, cooking and eating are much more important to a dwarf than hoards of gold. Dwarfs consume vast amounts of food, which never seems to make them fat, for they are hard workers, forever expending energy on their many activities. As one might expect, their food is the hearty, stick-to-the-rib type, and their cooking is reminiscent of the peasant cuisine of Europe or the cooking of the American colonies. Quantity is important, but food must also be delicious. The preparation of food is not strictly the domain of the female; everyone, from the king to young dwarf children, cooks. This is particularly true before festival time or any of the many parties and get-togethers that seem to

dominate dwarf life. With all the cooking, eating, and parties, it is a wonder that they have time to do anything else.

Dwarfs eat three meals and two snacks a day. Their main meal is served either in the morning or at midday. Snacks are eaten anytime from early morning to midafternoon, but never after the evening meal. There are, however, two exceptions — the Harvest Festival and the Spring Celebration — during which the festivities continue for seven days and seven nights. Dancing, singing, eating, and drinking, the dwarfs celebrate life to its fullest. Their lives are filled with poetry and song. Many of the great drinking songs known to humans are of dwarf origin.

The dwarf diet has great variety. Dwarfs consume all types of meat, vegetables, fruits, grains, legumes, and herbs, but not much fish. What they do not produce themselves they get by trading their crafts. Their food is cooked in iron pots and pans as well as some pottery vessels, all of which they make themselves.

Birthdays are not generally celebrated by dwarfs, probably because of their long life spans. However, for his 121st birthday a dwarf is given a celebration, and he or she may choose favorite dishes to be prepared by family and the many friends who will attend. A "small" party of fifty or so is planned — small for dwarfs but one that humans would think quite an undertaking! For example, after much deliberation this menu was chosen by a chieftain named Bucksnort.

MOLASSES MEAD

STUFFED APPLE TURKEY

CARROT BAKE

FOREST SALAD

TREE CAKE

LION'S TOOTH COFFEE

A typical dwarf breakfast is very hearty because most manual labor is completed before midday. Dwarfs are up at three or four A.M., so the morning is long. The breakfast menu might include the following, with a few additions depending on the season.

PIG CHOPS WITH GRAVY

BIRD EGGS

RICH MUSH

ROUND HEARTH CAKES

LUMP BREAD

FRUIT COBBLE WITH CLOTTED CREAM

LION'S TOOTH COFFEE

The special feature of a dwarf lunch is soup. A soup or stock pot is always simmering in the kitchen. Nothing is wasted. Bones are browned or not depending on the stock desired, and leftover vegetables are added, along with onions or leeks. A wide variety of foods are used to make soup or stock. One of the dwarfs' favorite soups is made in a flash from leftover salad, using a rich vegetable stock.

To make this unusual soup, bring the stock to a boil, then throw in leftover salad which has marinated in a vinaigrette salad dressing, and heat through. The greens must remain crunchy. The soup should be served hot. If you don't have a pot of stock simmering on the back burner of your stove, use boullion cubes to make the base.

Dwarfs eat all kinds of soup, but they do prefer hearty types. The recipe for such a soup follows. You can vary the ingredients according to your taste or what you have on hand.

POTTER'S CREAM SOUP

2 leeks	4 medium potatoes
2 ribs celery	1 cup fresh or frozen green
¾ pound broccoli	beans
3 carrots	1 bunch scallions
2 medium zucchini	¼ cup dried black mushrooms
1 medium rutabaga	¼ cup fresh chopped dill
2 medium white turnips	1 tablespoon salt
12 ounces fresh mushrooms	2 cups heavy cream,
4 Jerusalem artichokes	half-and-half, or milk
1 artichoke	

Clean the leeks and chop them coarsely, using only the white part. Wash, peel when necessary, and coarsely chop all the other vegetables and place them in a large pot with the dried mushrooms, dill, and salt. Add just enough water or vegetable stock to cover the vegetables. Bring to a boil and lower the heat. Simmer for about 1½ hours. Drain the cooked vegetables and reserve the liquid. Spoon the vegetables into a blender, processor, or food mill and puree. Return the pureed vegetables to the pot with the reserved cooking liquid and add the 2 cups of cream, half-and-half, or milk. Stir and heat through, but do not boil. Serve warm, garnished with more fresh chopped dill. Accompany with thick slices of bread.

Serves 5 dwarfs or 10 humans.

There is always a hum of activity in the dwarf kitchen. There may be large roasts in the oven or in a pot hanging in the fireplace, sides of

meats turning on a spit, and pies cooling on window sills, while pans of browned rolls are being brought out of the stone ovens. Delicious smells waft from the kitchen calling everyone to the table. It could not be more heavenly, and any dwarf would agree.

Roasted meat is the usual fare, but there are a few other dwarf specialties as well. Twice a year dwarfs go out on the lakes to fish for scootle fish. These taste very much like fresh-water perch. They are brought ashore and filleted. Naturally, it takes a lot of fillets to feed the dwarfs, but all the work is worth it. These little morsels are dipped in flour seasoned with salt and pepper (if they have it), and fried up in bacon fat. Nothing tastes grander.

The dwarfs' cuisine is synonymous with sausages of all types. Nothing is wasted. After butchering is completed, sausages are made with leftover meat. Dwarfs make sausages from chicken, turkey, pork, beef, and venison. The sausage may be smoked or eaten fresh. Links or patties are served at family meals, parties, and most definitely at major celebrations. No menu would be complete without sausages on the table.

The following sausage links are surprisingly easy to make, and with an investment of an hour or two you can have waiting in the freezer entrées for a few meals — assuming that your appetite doesn't match that of the dwarfs.

MAMMA ROCA'S SAUSAGE

1 package casings
5 pounds Boston butt or pork butt
5 teaspoons salt
5 teaspoons marjoram
1¼ to 2⅔ teaspoons pepper
3 small to medium onions, grated
½ cup water

Prepare the casings by washing off the salt they are packed in and soaking them overnight in water to soften them. Before stuffing the sausage, slip the opening of each casing over the water faucet and let warm water run gently through it. This will indicate if there are any holes in the casing. Cut the casing apart at the holes, otherwise the stuffing will be forced out.

Double grind the meat in a meat grinder or food processor, or have the butcher do it. Add the salt, marjoram, pepper, and onions to the meat and mix well. Add the water. In a skillet fry a small amount of the meat mixture to test for seasonings. Stuff the meat filling into the casings and tie off the links with string. This sausage is usually hung in a cool place to dry for a few hours or overnight. If you intend to dry the sausage, be sure you prepare it in cold weather.

Bring a large pot of water to a boil, then add the sausage links and simmer for 1½ hours. Serve them for breakfast, lunch, or dinner.

Freeze any remaining uncooked sausage in serving-size portions. It will keep for two months. Some dwarfs save the cooking liquid for soup stock, skimming off the fat first.

Serves 3 very hungry dwarfs or 10 to 12 humans.

This recipe is typical of the type of cooking done by the busy dwarfs. It is easy to put together and cooks on its own, or it can be made ahead of time and reheated. The dwarfs use a heavy Dutch oven for stewing, which they put in one of their stone ovens. They have two ovens, one inside their home next to the fireplace and one outside for use in warm weather.

Dwarf children learn all kinds of household tasks early in life, especially cooking. This recipe is a favorite of a pair of twins. They use it often. One browns the meat while the other chops the vegetables. Preparation takes a matter of minutes, and the recipe cooks in the oven without any attention.

DWARF DRUMSTICK STEW

4½ pounds of turkey legs (about 4 legs)
2 tablespoons safflower oil
12 ounces baby carrots
11 pearl onions
1 large onion, chopped
2 to 3 large ribs of celery, sliced
½ teaspoon salt
1 cup water

In a Dutch oven or casserole brown the turkey legs in the oil. Add all the vegetables and the salt and water. (Salt can be omitted, if desired.) Cover with a lid and place in a 375° oven for 2½ hours. When cooked, the drumsticks should be nice and brown with the meat falling off the bones.

For variety, add other vegetables, such as potatoes or green peppers. The peppers should be added about halfway through the cooking process. Turkey wings or thighs can be substituted for the legs.

Serves 2 dwarfs or 6 to 8 humans.

Dwarfs seldom have leftovers from their meals, but when there are leftovers, they use them imaginatively. The recipe that follows is an excellent way to use leftover turkey, chicken, duck, or even pork. This dish has a fruity flavor, which makes it interesting.

STUFFED APPLE TURKEY

4 slices of whole-wheat oatmeal, or other whole-grain bread
¼ cup coarsely chopped cashews or almonds
3 tablespoons butter
1 small onion, finely chopped
1 rib celery, finely chopped
¾ teaspoon poultry seasoning
2 teaspoons currant jelly
¼ cup orange juice
1½ to 2 cups cooked and chopped turkey
4 large baking apples
salt and pepper to taste
⅛ cup chicken or turkey stock, or vermouth (optional)

Preheat oven to 350°. Dice or coarsely chop the bread into ½-inch pieces. Place the bread in a bowl with the chopped nuts and set aside.

7

In a skillet melt the butter, then add the onion and celery. Sauté the vegetables until the onion is translucent but not brown. Add the poultry seasoning, then stir in 2 teaspoons of currant jelly, the orange juice, and broth. Mix the bread and turkey into the onion mixture and correct the seasoning with salt and pepper. Set aside.

Prepare the apples by cutting off about one-fourth of the apple at the stem end. Hollow out each apple with a small knife, leaving ¼ inch of apple next to the skin.

Fill the apples with the turkey mixture and place them in an ovenproof pan. Pour one tablespoon of stock, vermouth, or orange juice over each apple, and brush them with melted currant jelly. Add about ½ cup water or stock to the pan and cover with a lid or aluminum foil.

Bake them for 30 minutes. Remove the cover and allow the tops of the apples to brown. Brush them with additional melted jelly, if desired. The apples and stuffing can be prepared in advance and refrigerated, then assembled just before baking.

Serves one to 2 dwarfs or 4 humans.

For a hearty, winter party dish this is definitely the recipe. Dwarfs know how to entertain, so take a tip from them. They are especially fond of recipes that can be prepared ahead of time or those that cook on their own without much supervision. They love parties, but they are a busy, creative people whose days are completely filled with activity, much like humans nowadays.

RIBS À LA DWARF

6 to 8 large, meaty beef ribs (you could have them cut in half, but the dwarfs don't)
1⅔ cups dry red wine
½ cup hot water
½ teaspoon dried marjoram
½ teaspoon basil
1 large onion, sliced into ¼-inch rings
1 small bay leaf
1 teaspoon salt to taste
1 teaspoon pepper to taste
Arrowroot

In a Dutch oven, brown the ribs on all sides. Add the wine, hot water, herbs, and onion. Cover and simmer 1¼ hours. Add the salt and pepper and continue simmering for another 1¼ hours.

Remove the meat and keep warm. Skim the fat off the stock and reduce the liquid by one-third. Then thicken the reduced stock with arrowroot or cornstarch. Serve the ribs hot and pass the gravy separately.

This dish can be made ahead of time and reheated. It is even better the next day.

Serves one to 2 dwarfs, or 6 to 8 humans.

Although dwarf farmers raise domesticated animals, they also hunt, and both sexes are excellent shots. However, they kill only to eat and not for sport. For the Harvest Festival, venison sides traditionally are roasted over an open spit in the kitchen hearth. Outside in the pit ovens the dwarfs prepare many other courses for the festivities.

The following recipe is unusual in that it calls for wine. Small amounts of wine are produced by the dwarfs and customarily saved for special occasions such as birthdays, marriages, coming of age rites, and the miners' Spring Celebration.

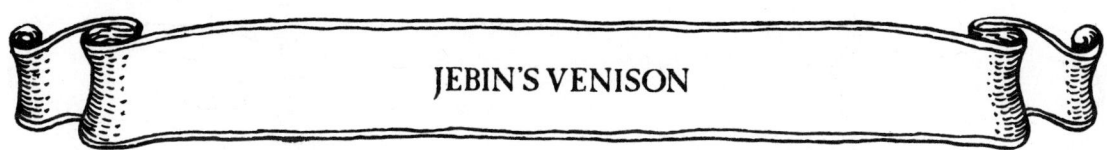

JEBIN'S VENISON

1½ tablespoons crushed black peppercorns
3 large or 4 small bay leaves
¾ teaspoon ground allspice
6 to 8 cloves
1½ cups brandy
1½ cups red wine
1½ cups vegetable oil
Venison roast (5 to 10 pounds)
Bacon for larding (optional)
Celery, carrots, and onions (amounts depend on size of meat)

9

Mix together the spices, brandy, wine, and oil to make a marinade. Place it in a glass or plastic container that is large enough to hold the venison and has a cover. A plastic bag is a very good container because there is no danger of spilling, and the meat can easily be turned periodically. Marinate the venison for at least 24 hours, although 2 to 3 days is better. The venison may be kept in the marinade for up to 2 weeks.

Remove the meat from the marinade and pat it dry. Either bard or lard the meat. Bacon can be used, but do not use too much or the bacon flavor will dominate.

Place the meat in a roasting pan with coarsely chopped carrots, celery, and onions. Pour one cup marinade over meat. Roast the venison 15 minutes per pound, basting every 10 to 15 minutes.

Remove the meat to a platter, arranging vegetables around the meat and keep warm.

Skim the fat from the drippings. Strain the remaining marinade and add it to the defatted drippings. Make a roux by stirring ½ cup flour into ½ cup melted butter. Add 2 cups of beef stock and the roux to the marinade. Serve this gravy in a separate gravy boat.

This is a very simple recipe; just remember to leave three days to one week for the meat to marinate. The recipe also works well with moose and elk. If you are cooking goat, substitute white wine for the red.

Serves 4 to 6.

The seat of learning for dwarf children is the kitchen. Through recipes they are taught the basics of weights, measures, arithmetic, reading, and writing. At the fireside they learn history and how to write poems or songs that will be performed at the festivals. Occasionally one or two families will gather together to teach music or carving. If someone in the community has a particular skill, such as beekeeping or pottery, the children will be sent to him or her to learn that skill.

Usually the first recipe used for teaching is one for yeast bread. Whole-grain yeast breads of all types are used because kneading the dough is fun. It is also good for developing the muscles in the hands, shoulders, and chest.

The following bread twists resemble the pretzels made by humans. Dwarfs enjoy them as snacks, and these twists are easy for them to carry in their pockets or bags. Rye Twists go well with the dark beer brewed by the dwarfs, and they are not too bad with beer brewed by humans, either.

BREADS

RYE TWISTS

1 package dry yeast or
1 yeast cake
1¼ cups warm water
2 teaspoons salt
1 teaspoon honey or sugar
2½ cups rye flour
1½ cups unbleached flour
1 egg mixed with 2 tablespoons water for an egg wash
Caraway seeds, celery seeds, or coarse salt

Proof the yeast in ¼ cup warm water in which one teaspoon sugar has been dissolved. In a bowl beat together the remaining cup of water, salt, and rye flour. Add the yeast mixture when it is foamy and add the unbleached flour, kneading until the dough is no longer sticky.

Let the dough rise in a warm place until it doubles in bulk. Punch it down, and form the dough into sticks or pretzel shapes. Place them on a greased sheet. Apply the egg wash and sprinkle the twists with seeds or coarse salt. Allow the twists to rise in a warm place until they are not quite double in bulk.

Preheat the oven to 475° and bake the twists for 10 minutes. Cool on a wire rack.

Makes 2 dozen rye twists.

This dwarf rye bread is not typical of rye bread in texture and taste. It is a slightly sweet bread with a soft crust. The celery seeds give the bread an interestingly different flavor.

SEEDED RYE BREAD

2 cups milk
1 package dry yeast or 1 yeast cake
1 teaspoon honey or sugar
3¼ cups rye flour
½ cup turbinado sugar or dark brown sugar
2½ teaspoons salt
2½ tablespoons vegetable oil
2¼ to 3¼ cups unbleached flour (or half whole-wheat and half unbleached; this will produce a slightly heavier loaf), or gluten flour can be used
2 teaspoons celery seeds
2 tablespoons cornmeal

In a saucepan scald the milk, cool it to 105° to 115° and dissolve the yeast in the milk. Add one teaspoon of honey or sugar. Proof the yeast by putting it in a warm place until the yeast mixture becomes foamy.

In a bowl combine the rye flour along with the yeast-milk mixture, sugar, salt, and oil. Beat well with an electric mixer or by hand. Gradually add the unbleached flour until a sticky dough is formed. Add the celery seeds.

Remove the dough from the bowl, place it on a floured surface, and continue to knead in the remaining flour until the dough is stiff and easy to handle. Place it in a bowl, cover with a clean cloth, and allow it to rise until it is double in size (for about 2 hours).

Punch down the dough. Divide it into 2 equal portions and shape into oval loaves. Place them on a well-greased baking sheet covered with the cornmeal. Grease the tops of the loaves and allow them to rise for about one hour.

Bake at 400° for 15 minutes, then lower the temperature to 350° for 20 to 30 minutes. To test for doneness, tap the bottom of the loaves; if they sound hollow, the bread is done. Cool on a wire rack. The bread may be served warm or cold.

Makes 2 loaves. Serves one dwarf.

A favorite of the dwarfs is Lump Bread, so called because it is baked as a lump in the oven. Because of the simplicity of its preparation, this bread is served often and is always the main bread at large parties, as well as at daily meals. Although Lump Bread is featured, no meal would be complete without several types of bread on the table.

Lump bread is served whole and at the table everyone breaks off as much as he wants. Of course it can also be sliced. Indentations made in the raw dough before it is baked make it easier to break the bread into sections after it is cooked.

LUMP BREAD

3 cups whole-wheat flour
1½ cups unbleached flour
¼ cup gluten flour or ¼ cup unbleached flour
2 teaspoons Vegesal or salt
1½ teaspoons baking soda
3 to 4 tablespoons butter
2 cups buttermilk or sour milk

Preheat the oven to 400°.

In a bowl, thoroughly mix all the dry ingredients together, using a wire whisk or fork. Cut in the butter with two knives, a pastry blender or, if you want to be authentically dwarf, use your fingers and rub the flour mixture with the butter between your thumb and first two fingers.

When the mixture resembles coarse cornmeal, add the buttermilk and mix (dough should be lumpy). Form the dough into one lump and drop it onto a greased and floured baking sheet. Bake the bread for 25 to 30 minutes. Thoroughly baked bread should have a hollow sound when tapped.

Serves 6 to 8 humans or 2 to 4 dwarfs.

Corn, a staple in the dwarf diet, is the main ingredient in this much-loved recipe for Round Hearth Cakes. Delicious hot off the griddle or frying pan, the cakes are split horizontally and filled with meat or spread with fruit jam. This bread is also eaten cold by the dwarfs when they work in the fields or down in the mines. These cakes are almost always found on the breakfast table because the easy-to-prepare mixture is made ahead of time and then cooked into cakes just before serving.

ROUND HEARTH CAKES

2 cups cornmeal
2 teaspoons vegetable salt
1½ cups boiling water
¼ cup whole-wheat flour
2 tablespoons butter

Place all the ingredients in a saucepan, and heat until the mixture thickens. Cook for one minute after the mixture starts to bubble. Stir constantly to prevent sticking. Remove the batter from the heat, cover, and let it stand for one hour or longer.

Just before eating, scoop out some of the mixture and form it into round cakes. They can be any size, but 3 or 4 inches in diameter is about right.

Fry the cakes on a greased griddle over moderate heat until they are golden brown. These are best when hot, but they can also be eaten at room temperature.

Makes about 6 or 8 pieces, enough for one dwarf.

HARVEST BREAD

½ cup brown rice meal
½ cup cornmeal
⅓ cup whole-wheat or unbleached flour
½ teaspoon salt
2 teaspoons baking powder
1 cup milk
1 egg, beaten
3 tablespoons melted butter
1 tablespoon honey (optional)

Preheat the oven to 450°.

In a bowl combine the rice and corn meals, flour, salt, and baking powder. In another bowl mix together the milk, egg, melted butter, and honey, if desired. Add the milk mixture to the dry ingredients and mix well.

Pour the batter into a greased 8-inch square baking pan. Bake for 20 to 25 minutes.

Serves 4 to 6 humans, one to 2 dwarfs

NOTE: Rice meal is easily made in a blender or coffee mill by grinding brown rice until powdery.

To a dwarf, courting means observing a traditional ritual that may, and usually does, last for years. The choice is more or less the right of the individual. However, parents play an important role in the decision, and their advice is always sought out and usually taken. For the loving and loyal dwarfs, marriage lasts a lifetime, and selection of a mate is a most important decision. From the moment their courting begins, the couple will always be in the company of family and friends. Their only opportunity for "private" conversation will be while dancing together at parties or sitting under the Courting Tree. Even then they will be in full view of everyone, for the tree is in the village square. The seat of the Courting Tree is built into the hollow of two intertwining live oaks. The ornately carved seat was lovingly hewn by dwarf artisans. Here countless couples have whispered the secrets of their hearts to each other.

Another tradition, the courting bread, is also observed. After the longest courtship in dwarf history, Magda finally won the heart of Cully when she baked the following bread for him to taste at dinner. It is now customary for this bread to be served at least once during a courtship. There is, however, a story of one young hopeful who served it every time she had her beau for dinner. It is said he finally married her just so she would stop making the courting bread.

THE COURTING BREAD

1½ cups unbleached flour
½ cup ground oatmeal
1 teaspoon baking powder
½ teaspoon baking soda
1 teaspoon salt (preferably Vegesal)
⅛ to ¼ teaspoon nutmeg (freshly grated, if possible)
½ cup softened butter
½ cup turbinado sugar or brown sugar
2 eggs
1¼ cups apple, ground with peel
½ cup grated sharp cheddar cheese
¼ cup chopped nuts or sunflower seeds

Preheat the oven to 350°.

Using a wire whisk, mix the flours, baking powder, baking soda, salt, and nutmeg. Set the mixture aside.

In another bowl cream the butter with the sugar until it is fluffy. Beat in the eggs one at a time. This mixture should be light.

Add the apples, cheese, and sunflower seeds. Stir in the flour mixture only until just blended. Do not overmix.

Pour the dough into a greased, floured 9 × 5 × 3-inch loaf pan. Bake one hour or until done.

Makes one loaf with which to win a heart.

The climate in the dwarf village of Verderoc does not provide a long growing season. This, however, is no problem for the industrious dwarfs, who with their productive gardens and bountiful fields produce a surplus of crops. They dry, pickle, can, and put into cold storage all excess produce for the winter months. They were the first to invent the greenhouse principle for growing simple greens for salad in the winter months. Dwarfs also sprout seeds and beans of all types to be used all year round.

During the growing season vegetables are served plain, cooked only with a few herbs and butter or oil. Dwarfs also combine several vegetables and steam them to a crunchy tenderness. Occasionally, special vegetable dishes are prepared, but the dwarfs usually spend more time preparing the main course and dessert. Still, there are no less than two vegetables served at the main meal, and this does not include the salad, which is always served.

Strictly speaking, this is not a recipe prepared only by the dwarfs but is a salad dressing used by just about anyone who can get his hands on peanuts. Tradition has it that it was invented by an elf.

 **SALAD DRESSING À LA PEANUT**

¾ cup oil
¼ cup vinegar
2 tablespoons honey
1 teaspoon garlic powder
1 teaspoon onion powder
1 teaspoon salt
¼ teaspoon pepper
3 to 4 teaspoons crunchy-style peanut butter

Place all the above ingredients in blender and blend.

This dressing is especially nice on a spinach salad; but any green salad will do.

Makes 1 ¼ cups.

Human gardeners always seem to have an abundance of squash in their garden patches. Dwarfs would consider that a cause for celebration. The beautiful dwarf gardens are very productive. Dwarfs love squash and prepare it in endless ways. It is said that the vegetable cakes and breads humans eat today are of dwarf origin.

This recipe for Squash Boats is only one of the dwarfs' many stuffed-squash recipes. These zucchini "boats" have the earthy flavor of mushrooms.

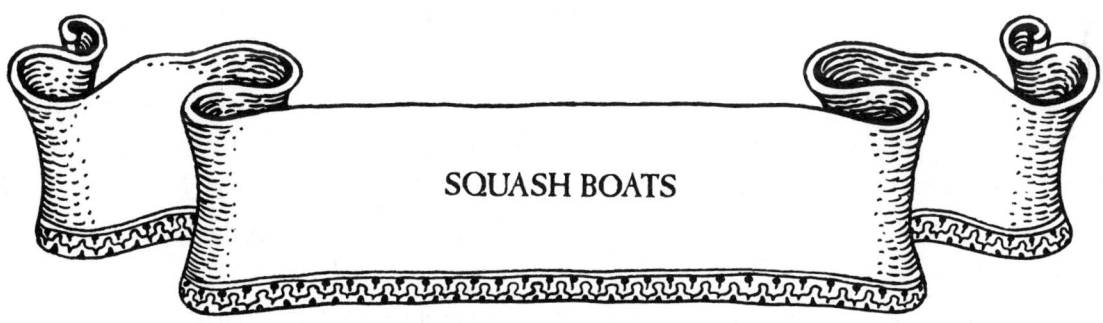

SQUASH BOATS

6 small zucchini or yellow squash
5 or 6 medium-size mushrooms
1 very small center stalk of celery
1 small onion
2 tablespoons butter
Pinch of marjoram
¼ teaspoon thyme
1 tablespoon sesame seeds
Salt to taste
5 grinds of pepper
1 biscuit of shredded wheat
2 tablespoons heavy cream

Preheat the oven to 350°.

Scoop out the meat of the squash with a spoon or melon baller and reserve.

Chop the mushrooms, celery, onion, and squash meat fine, or use a food processor. Melt the butter in saucepan and sauté the vegetables. Add the marjoram, thyme, sesame seeds, salt, and pepper. Crush the shredded wheat biscuit and add it along with the heavy cream.

Fill the squash boats and bake them in an ovenproof dish for about 15 to 20 minutes.

The Squash Boats can be prepared ahead and baked just before serving. For a completely different taste, try this recipe without the mushrooms.

Serves 6 humans or 1 dwarf.

If you think no one will eat cooked greens, try the recipe that the dwarf children love. It is made with beet greens, but any greens or green vegetable can be used.

DWARF GREENS

10 ounces of kale, spinach, or other greens
1 large onion chopped fine
2 cloves garlic
1 medium green pepper
1½ cups fresh tomatoes, peeled and chopped fine, or 1 cup tomato puree plus ⅓ cup water
¼ to ⅓ pound nitrate-free bacon, fried crisply

Cut the cooked bacon into small pieces. Reserve 3 to to 4 tablespoons of the bacon fat. Set both aside.

Wash the kale and remove the tough ribs. Tear the leaves into medium-size pieces.

Dice the onions, garlic, and green pepper, and mix them with the diced peeled tomatoes. Salt and pepper the vegetables to taste.

In a heatproof casserole, alternate layers of greens with the onion-tomato mixture, starting with the greens and ending with the onion-tomato mixture. There should be at least four layers. Sprinkle the top with the bacon pieces and bacon grease. Cover and cook over low heat for 45 to 60 minutes.

Try this recipe with other vegetables such as finely chopped broccoli, cauliflower, or beet greens.

Serves one dwarf or 4 to 5 humans.

Considering all the food served at each meal, it would seem impossible for dwarfs also to want dessert, but they do. Dessert is always served, even at breakfast. It may not always be a pie or cake. Dessert could mean a bowl of cut fresh fruit, or sliced apples cooked with a sauce, or even honey butter on a piece of bread. (It would be more like a loaf of bread, or at the very least half a loaf!) At any rate, dessert is a must.

This recipe would satisfy a crowd of humans, but it would only take care of three dwarfs. Custard is an all-time dwarf favorite because it can be made in large quantities with little effort.

DESSERTS

DWARF'S CUSTARD

3 teaspoons vanilla extract or 2 teaspoons vanilla and 1 teaspoon almond extract.
⅛ teaspoon salt
⅔ to ¾ cup honey (depending on the sweetness you desire)
12 to 16 eggs (more eggs will make the custard firmer)
8 cups milk, hot

Preheat the oven to 325°.

In a large bowl combine the vanilla, honey, and eggs. If you use raw milk, scald it. Stir the hot milk into the eggs very gradually while beating.

Strain the mixture through a sieve and pour it into custard cups. Place the cups in pan filled with one inch of hot water.

Bake for 40 minutes, or until a knife inserted in the custard comes out clean. The dwarfs, however, do not put the custard cups in hot water. They put the custard into heavy bowls and place them directly in the oven. The custard is not as tender but tastes just as good.

Serve the custard warm or ice cold. Dwarfs insist on eating their custard with heavy or whipped cream.

Serves 16 humans or 3 dwarfs.

A fruit cobble, as it is called, is a mainstay all year long. Using fruits that are in season, the cobble is varied. The topping is changed to produce what humans call a crisp or a betty. This particular recipe is usually served to guests during apple season. The same recipe can be used for any fruit by adjusting the amount of honey to the tartness of the fruit.

DWARF FRUIT COBBLE

½ to ⅔ cup honey
1½ tablespoon cornstarch or arrowroot
4 large winesap apples, peeled and sliced (about 4½ cups)
¼ teaspoon allspice
¼ teaspoon cinnamon
(optional)
2 cups fresh cranberries, chopped coarsely
1 tablespoon water
2 tablespoons butter
Topping (recipe follows)

Preheat the oven to 400°.

Mix the honey, cornstarch or arrowroot, apples, spices, cranberries, and water together in an ovenproof casserole. Cook over medium-low heat just until the liquid thickens. Remove from the stove.

Spread the topping over the fruit mixture in the casserole, covering it completely. Bake for 25 to 35 minutes. Serve warm or cold, as is or with cream, whipped cream, or ice cream.

Serves 2 dwarfs or 6 humans.

BISCUIT TOPPING

1½ cups whole-wheat pastry flour
1½ teaspoons baking powder
¼ teaspoon salt
4 tablespoons butter
¼ cup honey, brown sugar, or turbinado sugar
⅓ cup milk

Blend together the flour, baking powder, and salt. Cut in the butter with two knives or a pastry blender until the mixture is crumbly.

Mix together the honey or sugar and milk, and add it all at once to the flour mixture. Blend only until mixed. Do not overmix.

The hills on the outskirts of Verderoc are the site for the Sparrow Mine and Studgat Memorial Biyearly Fair and Exhibit. Dwarfs from near and far display their wares, exhibit their skills, buy and trade goods, and compete for prizes. Needless to say, cooking is one of the major competitions. In the adolescent division of the 125th Biyearly Fair a young girl named Wilga won first prize for her pie crust. She subsequently became one of the judges of the fair many years later. Wilga's is a good basic recipe, and, what's even better, it never fails. If you happen to own a food processor, it could not be easier.

WILGA'S CRUST

1½ cups flour (any combination of unbleached and whole-wheat)
¼ teaspoon salt
¼ cup lard and ¼ cup butter or ½ cup lard or ½ cup butter
2 tablespoons beaten egg
1 teaspoon honey or raw sugar (optional)
1½ to 2 tablespoons water or orange or lemon juice

Process the flour, salt and shortening in a processor with a steel blade, and add the egg, honey, and water or juice through the tube. Run the processor until a ball of dough is formed. Chill the dough or use it immediately.

If you are not using a processor, cut the lard and butter into the flour until the mixture resembles coarse meal.

In another bowl mix the honey, water, or juice and egg together with a fork.

Add the honey mixture to the flour and form a ball. Chill the dough or use it immediately.

If the dough is used as a crust for meat, cheese or any other savory dish, omit the honey.

Makes one 9-inch pie crust.

NOTE: If orange or lemon juice is used, add a pinch of baking soda to the dry ingredients. The addition of the citrus juice and baking soda makes a more tender crust. The dwarfs most often use this version of the crust.

Whether they are working or playing, dwarfs know how to have a good time and enjoy each situation to the fullest. From childhood on they are taught simple ways to make a game out of the most difficult task by singing a song, asking others to help with the work, or finding a way to compete with themselves as they work alone. For example, every year a game is made of gathering fruit or nuts for a favorite dessert. This task is usually relegated to the dwarf children. But when it comes to nut pie, the adults compete in the hunt, and the one who collects and cracks the most nuts gets the first pie out of the oven.

The following recipes are not exclusively the dwarfs'. Fairies, elves, and giants also make the nut pie and tree cake, but none have as much fun collecting the nuts as the dwarfs.

NUT PIE

1 unbaked 9-inch pie shell, homemade, frozen, or from a mix (*see preceding recipe*)
⅛ to ¼ cup wheat germ (optional)
3 large eggs, well beaten
1¼ cups maple syrup
¼ cup honey
1 teaspoon vanilla
¼ teaspoon vegetable salt or sea salt
⅔ to 1 cup pecans, walnuts, filberts, or other nuts

Preheat the oven to 425°.
Have ready one unbaked pie shell. If you are using a packaged mix, add ⅛ to ¼ cup of wheat germ to make it more flavorful and nutritious. If you are using a frozen shell, it is best to sprinkle

one tablespoon of wheat germ on it and press it into the crust with your fingers or the back of a spoon.

To make the filling, beat the eggs in a bowl and add the maple syrup, honey, vanilla, and salt. Mix the ingredients thoroughly. Add the nuts and mix them in. Pour the filling into the shell. Bake the pie for 30 to 40 minutes. It may be served warm or ice-cold as is or with heavy cream or ice cream.

This pie is very easy to make, but it can be expensive unless you have a free supply of nuts.

Serves 2 dwarfs or 8 to 10 humans.

This cake was first made as a present for the Wizard's coming of age party in Azuria, the fairy city. The dwarfs, of course, presented many gifts but the young wizard seemed to enjoy this the best. Since then it has been a very special cake in Verderoc.

TREE CAKE

7 eggs, separated
1 cup maple syrup
1 teaspoon vanilla
1 cup plus 2 tablespoons potato starch
2 teaspoons baking powder
Pinch of salt
½ teaspoon cream of tartar
½ cup walnuts, finely chopped
Whipped cream
Bitter chocolate or carob

Preheat the oven to 350°.

Beat the egg yolks until they are lemon-yellow and very thick. Add the maple syrup, vanilla, potato starch, and baking powder.

Beat the egg whites; when they foam add the salt and cream of tartar.

Fold one-third of the egg yolk mixture into the egg whites. Then fold in the remaining egg-yolk batter and the nuts.

Pour the batter into a 10-inch tube pan. Bake at 350° for the first 20 minutes; reduce temperature to 325° and continue baking for 55 minutes.

Cool the cake upside down on a rack. When it has thoroughly cooled, remove it from the pan. Cut the cake horizontally into four rounds.

Frost between each layer as well as the entire outside of the cake with maple-sweetened whipped cream. Sprinkle the top with shaved bitter chocolate or carob. Keep refrigerated.

Serves one dwarf.

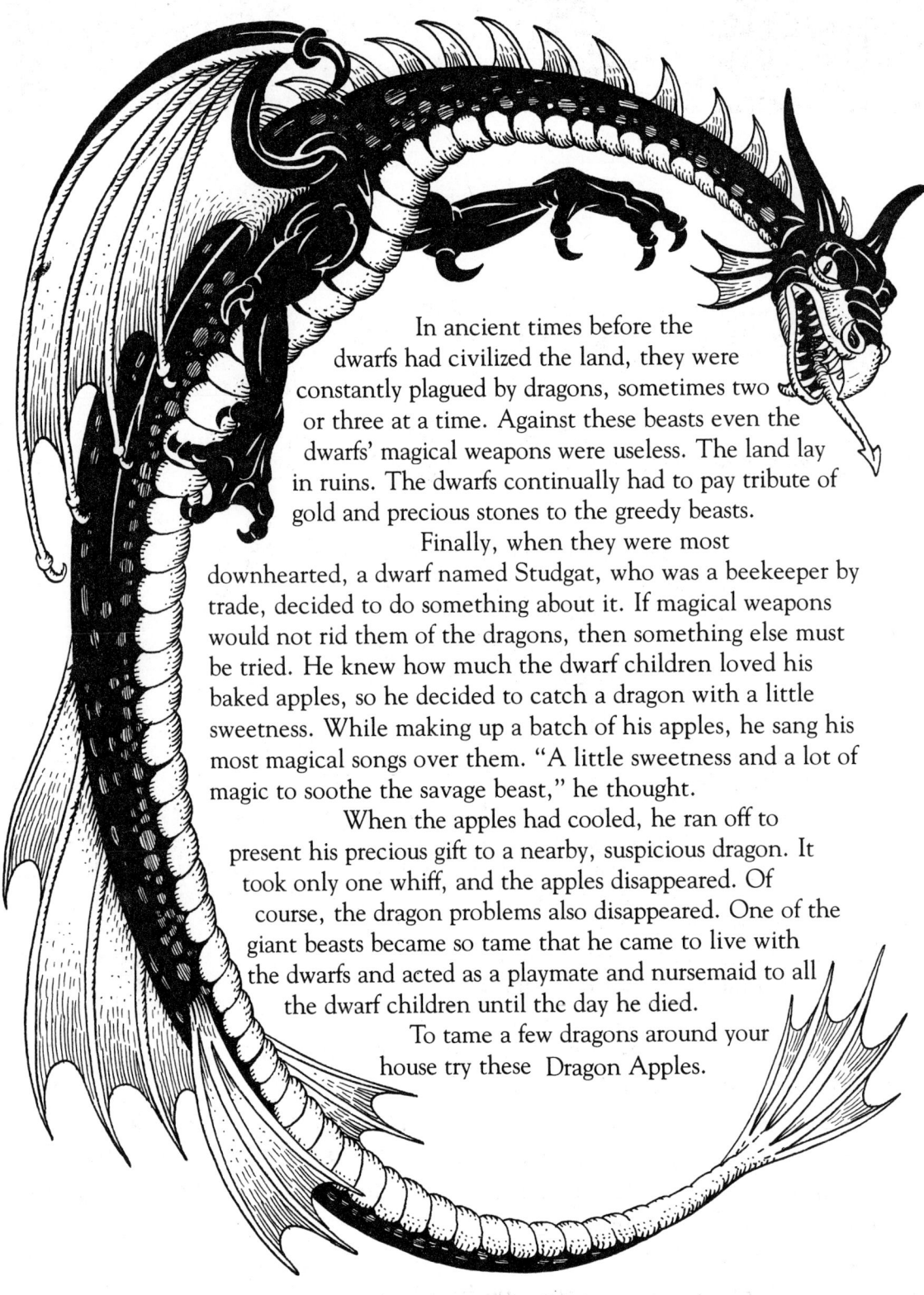

In ancient times before the dwarfs had civilized the land, they were constantly plagued by dragons, sometimes two or three at a time. Against these beasts even the dwarfs' magical weapons were useless. The land lay in ruins. The dwarfs continually had to pay tribute of gold and precious stones to the greedy beasts.

Finally, when they were most downhearted, a dwarf named Studgat, who was a beekeeper by trade, decided to do something about it. If magical weapons would not rid them of the dragons, then something else must be tried. He knew how much the dwarf children loved his baked apples, so he decided to catch a dragon with a little sweetness. While making up a batch of his apples, he sang his most magical songs over them. "A little sweetness and a lot of magic to soothe the savage beast," he thought.

When the apples had cooled, he ran off to present his precious gift to a nearby, suspicious dragon. It took only one whiff, and the apples disappeared. Of course, the dragon problems also disappeared. One of the giant beasts became so tame that he came to live with the dwarfs and acted as a playmate and nursemaid to all the dwarf children until the day he died.

To tame a few dragons around your house try these Dragon Apples.

DRAGON APPLES

4 large cooking apples
½ cup ground almonds, filberts, pecans, or other nuts
1 tablespoon cinnamon
½ cup raisins
⅛ teaspoon freshly ground nutmeg (optional)
4 to 8 tablespoons honey
4 teaspoons butter
½ cup boiling water

Preheat the oven to 400°.

Wash the apples and remove core to within ¼ inch of the bottom. Remove a strip of apple peel from the cored end. Hollow out each apple to make an opening large enough to accommodate the stuffing. Chop the extra apple finely and set aside. Combine the nuts, cinnamon, raisins, and nutmeg. Fill the centers of the apples with this mixture. Top each apple with one to 2 tablespoons of honey and dot with butter. Place them in a baking pan and add ½ cup boiling water and reserved chopped apple to the pan. Cover and bake for 25 to 45 minutes. Serve the apples warm or cold with the pan juices and heavy cream.

Serves one dwarf or 4 humans or one baby dragon.

Dwarfs eat no chocolate, but they do have something similar in taste called carob. Unlike chocolate, carob has its own natural sweetness. Using carob, the dwarfs make a candy *without* any sweetening of any kind. This candy is a favorite snack of the dwarfs, and they consume great quantities. It is given to the dwarf children almost without restriction because it is good for them.

When making this candy consider that the quality of the finished product depends on the quality of the ingredient, because there isn't any sweetening to mask the taste. Therefore, buy the best. It is great for those on sugar-restricted diets. Human children love it, too.

DWARF CAROB CANDY

4 tablespoons butter
4 tablespoons coconut oil
4 tablespoons almond oil or apricot oil
2 tablespoons lecithin granules

1 to 1¼ cups nonfat dry milk
1 cup carob powder
1½ to 2 teaspoons vanilla
1 cup chopped nuts (optional)
½ cup raisins (optional)

Combine the butter, oils, lecithin granules, and powdered milk in a saucepan over low to medium heat and stir until the butter is melted and the ingredients are thoroughly mixed.

Remove the pan from the heat. Combine the carob powder, the butter-and-milk mixture, and the vanilla in a blender or food processor. This may have to be done in two batches, depending on the power of the blender.

Remove the mixture from the blender and knead it for a few seconds. At this point the nuts or raisins may be added. Divide the mixture into serving portions or form it into candy-bar shapes. Place in the refrigerator to harden. It's ready to serve when hard.

The candy may also be placed in very small paper or foil nut cups and topped with coconut or a roasted almond.

Serves one dwarf or 6 to 8 humans.

Nothing goes together like parties, songs, drink, food, and dwarfs. Beer and mead are the most popular drinks among the adults. In the mornings and on very cold days Lion's Tooth Coffee is served.

Dwarfs grow an herb plant with leaves like those of rosemary but with purple flowers resembling those of the chive. The herb is called Lion's Tooth, and it is the root of this plant that is dried, ground, and roasted to produce the "coffee" that dwarfs drink.

Dandelion root is very similar in taste to Lion's Tooth. You can purchase dandelion roots in specialty shops and health-food stores, but there is no reason why you cannot dig them out of your lawn, wash, dry, roast, and grind them yourself.

LION'S TOOTH COFFEE

1 teaspoon dried roasted dandelion root

8 ounces water

Place the water in a saucepan, add the dandelion root, and bring to a boil. Simmer for 5 minutes.

Strain and serve the drink with honey or cream if desired.

If you add roasted chicory root in proportions of ¼ part chicory to one part dandelion root, the taste is even better.

For another variation roast barley and grind it in a mill or blender, then brew it as above. It makes an interesting coffee substitute. A commercially prepared product is also available.

Makes one cup.

The dwarfs serve this traditional drink at most meals and always at the Harvest Festival. To the dwarfs it symbolizes the forming of their society. There are many variations of this recipe; but this is the original.

MOLASSES MEAD

1 cup tupelo honey
½ teaspoon ground ginger
½ cup light molasses
¾ cup vinegar
2 quarts cold water
1 teaspoon baking soda

Place the honey, ginger, molasses, and vinegar in an enamel or stainless-steel saucepan and cook over medium heat until all the ingredients are blended. Do not boil. Pour the mead into a jar to cool. Refrigerate if desired.

When you are ready to serve the mead, add the water and mix thoroughly. Stir in the baking soda for fizz. Serve at once, with or without ice.

You may substitute 2 quarts sparkling water for the baking soda and plain water.

Serves 2 dwarfs or 6 humans.

The favorite drink among dwarf children is Milk Nog. It is often made without spices, because spices must be obtained through trade and are often very expensive. Often rose water or even anise is used to flavor the nog. The children drink this nog or molasses mead as a snack with bread or crackers.

SPICED DWARF NOG

4 eggs, separated
1 teaspoon vanilla
¼ to ⅓ cup honey
¼ teaspoon cinnamon
¼ teaspoon nutmeg
Dash of allspice
2 cups milk
1 cup heavy cream

Beat the egg whites until stiff but not dry. In another bowl, using the same beaters, beat the egg yolks until they are light and lemon-colored.

Add the vanilla, then the honey, and continue beating.

Add the cinnamon, nutmeg, allspice, milk, and heavy cream. Continue to beat until thoroughly blended; then fold in the egg whites.

Ladle the nog into cups and sprinkle the surface with allspice or nutmeg. For humans this makes a great nonalcoholic eggnog at Christmas.

Serves one to 2 dwarf children or 4 to 6 humans.

Dwarfs possess a rare combination of qualities. They are earthy yet childlike, hardworking but full of fun, rugged but tender. These are a happy and prosperous people; they radiate what humans call the joy of life.

THE AMAZONS

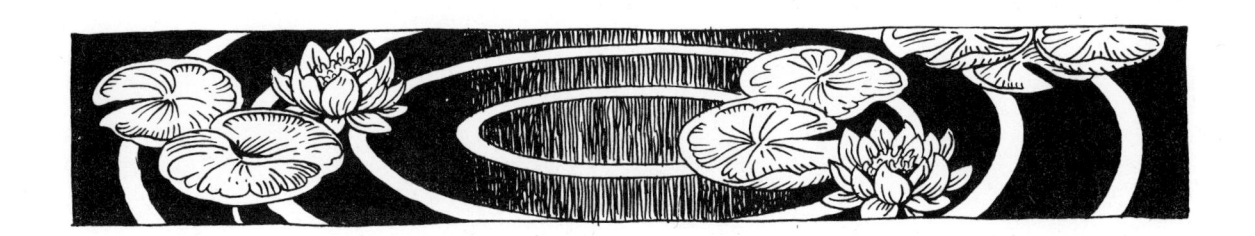

At sunset on the winter solstice, while snow-white pegases mount the sky, the high priestess, Dila, presides over the festival of sunlight. Dressed in bright ceremonial robes, the regal priestess recounts to her fellow Amazons the saga of their escape from the island of Nor Bodo, their landing on the shores of Zir, and the women's subsequent friendship with the flying horses. The sun sets, and torches are lit as the high priestess ends her historical chant. Now the signal is given to begin the traditional songs and dances and to bring out the food for an elaborate banquet, which is presented dish by dish with great pomp. This ceremony has been performed countless times. The women never tire of recounting the day when they were befriended by the magnificent snow-white pegasus who brought them to this lush desert oasis with its magical spring. The woman named the fertile region along with its spring Sizaeo. Their new home provided everything the Amazons needed — their food, strength, prolonged youth, and amazing mental powers.

Using their mental powers and their extraordinary strength, the women built an ornate circular city. Their homes skirt the edge of a lush oasis. In the center a small lake is fed by an underground spring, and in the middle of the lake stands a palacelike structure, which functions as a ceremonial and recreation center. No one lives in this building, and it can only be reached by three bridges or by boat. A high priestess and five other women compose the Council of Maidens, which rules for a decade. During this time the priestess functions as guardian of the spring, coordinator of the work schedule, and chief planner of recreation and ceremonial feasts.

Although the Amazons live a long life in their secluded oasis, they are happy, childlike women who are high-spirited and dauntlessly competitive. They can innocently enjoy hide-and-seek or some other harmless game, but they also have athletic prowess and an aggressive nature that would be envied by any warrior or Olympic champion. These women are mental giants with extraordinary psychic powers that move mountains or transmit messages to the wizard's distant mountaintop. On the other hand, they are touched by a beautiful sunset or a flower swaying in the breeze. The women did not call themselves Amazons. That name was given to them by their only welcomed and frequent visitor, the wizard Alzar, who told them that the name means "perfection from the waters." To humans the word Amazon has come to mean "woman warrior."

Every Amazon must take her turn working in the fields and orchards. The day begins before dawn and ends at noon. Those who are not assigned to the fields work at home and cook the meal that is brought to the field-workers at daybreak. By noon the main meal of the day is prepared, and all the Amazons wash and dress for this leisurely repast. A period of rest follows. Some nap, others pursue weaving, jewelry making, or pottery; still others write poems and music. In the afternoon they return to various chores necessary to repair and maintain their homes and communal buildings. When night comes, the Amazons eat a light meal, then study astronomy, architecture, and philosophy or play games. They always end the evenings's activities with some form of meditation to restore their strength.

Their society has discovered a perfect balance between mind and body. In order to maintain their strength the women take a great interest in food. Amazons generally eat five times a day. Their larger meals are eaten at dawn and noon; the other three are more like snacks. But during the festival or at athletic competitions, feasts are arranged by the high priestess.

Those women who work in the field eat their first meal, a snack of sliced fruit, and a turnover of mild cheese with spiced herb tea, upon rising. At dawn the field-workers are brought their morning meal in picnic baskets. There is a meat dish, perhaps chicken livers, or a vegetable pie, such as Zucchini-Leek Pie, accompanied by bread and iced herb tea or a special papaya drink.

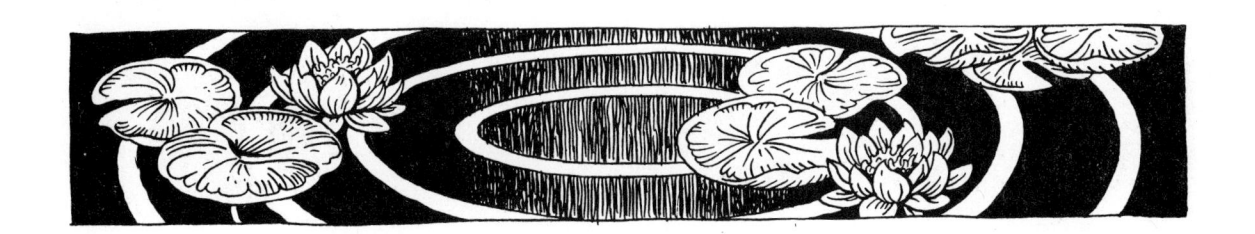

At lunch the Amazons relax and dine elegantly. The table is set with intricately woven tablecloths and napkins, colorful pottery, and eating implements made of bone. A typical meal might include Fish à la Oasis, Wild Duck with Gravy, rice with nuts, and a choice of vegetables and breads, followed by black cake with herb tea or fruit juice and, occasionally, some wine.

Their evening meal is very light. It may be only fruit salad with muffins or perhaps leftovers from an earlier meal.

Before bedtime the women may have a fruit punch or iced herb tea and bread, or a piece of fruit.

The Amazons have always been secretive about the location of their oasis. The first news of their existence came from a dwarf child who was innocently given a ride to Sizaeo by a young pegasus. Although the women responded to the child with motherly warmth because they knew he meant them no harm, they were fearful that others might follow. The young pegasus was rebuked for his action.

However, this first encounter heralded the beginning of a trade route between the Amazons and the dwarfs. The child went home on a flying horse laden with exotic foods and spices. The dwarfs were so pleased with the return of the child that they, in turn, sent wines, foods, and valuable metals. The dwarfs are not allowed in Sizaeo and the Amazons very rarely visit them, but trade has continued by way of the pegases.

When the child landed in Sizaeo, one of the meals he was served featured a bird soup, in this case, Duck Soup.

DUCK SOUP

1 4½-pound duck, cut into serving pieces and giblets
1 large onion, coarsely chopped
1 stalk of celery, chopped
6 to 12 prunes, pitted
⅓ cup vinegar
¼ cup sugar or honey
Salt
White pepper to taste

Place the duck and its giblets in a large pot. Add the onion, celery, and enough water to cover the duck. Bring the water to a boil, skimming off the froth to keep the broth clear. Add the prunes and simmer for 1½ hours.

Let the soup stand until it is cool. Refrigerate overnight, if possible. Remove all the fat from the surface of the soup.

When ready to serve, reheat and add ⅓ cup vinegar and ¼ cup sugar or honey. When the soup is thoroughly heated, season and serve over homemade noodles (*recipe follows*).

Serves 6 to 8 humans or 2 to 3 Amazons.

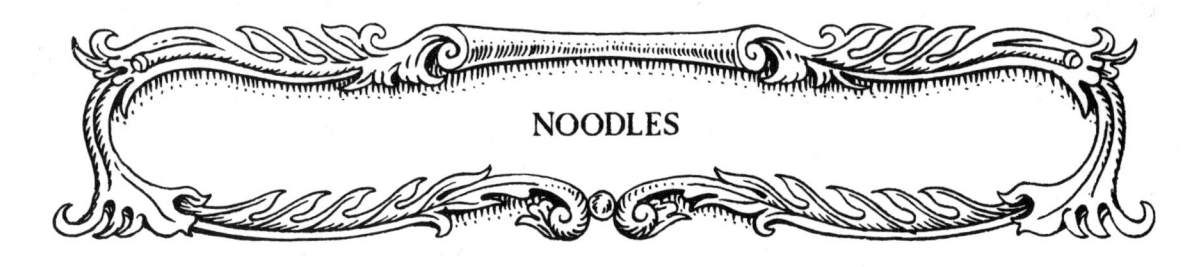

NOODLES

3 cups flour (unbleached, soya-carob flour or ½ unbleached and ½ whole-wheat)
4 to 5 eggs
1 teaspoon water

Mix all the ingredients together and knead until the dough is no longer sticky. Divide the dough into pieces and roll out thin on a floured surface. Cut it into thin strips.

Drop the noodles into salted, boiling water. After the noodles rise to the surface, cook them two to three minutes. Drain and serve.

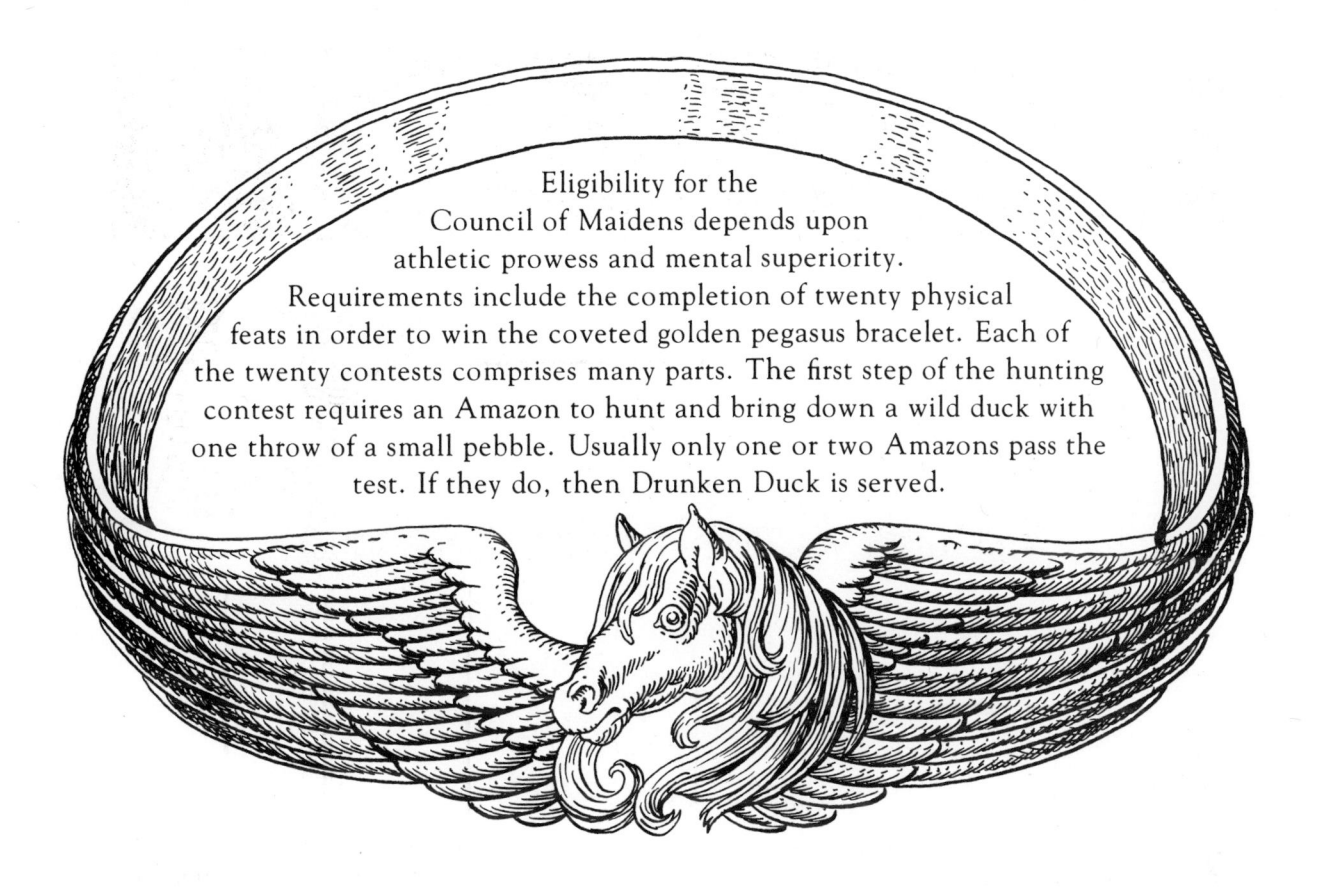

Eligibility for the Council of Maidens depends upon athletic prowess and mental superiority. Requirements include the completion of twenty physical feats in order to win the coveted golden pegasus bracelet. Each of the twenty contests comprises many parts. The first step of the hunting contest requires an Amazon to hunt and bring down a wild duck with one throw of a small pebble. Usually only one or two Amazons pass the test. If they do, then Drunken Duck is served.

WILD DRUNKEN DUCK

2 cups red burgundy
1 bay leaf
3 cloves garlic
8 whole black peppercorns
1 wild duck or wild goose
Bacon or leaf lard for barding
Apples
Onions

Make a marinade with the burgundy, bay leaf, and garlic.

Marinate the duck for one or 2 days by placing it in the marinade in a tightly sealed plastic bag. Turn the duck a few times a day so that the marinade will be absorbed evenly.

Preheat the oven to 325°.

To roast the duck, drain and reserve the marinade. Bard the duck thoroughly with the bacon or strips of leaf lard, especially on the breast. Stuff the cavity with apples and onions. Roast 20 to 25 minutes per pound until desired doneness.

Amazons like their duck well done, but it can be served pink. Trolls eat duck rare. Serve with Gravy.

Serves one Amazon or 4 humans.

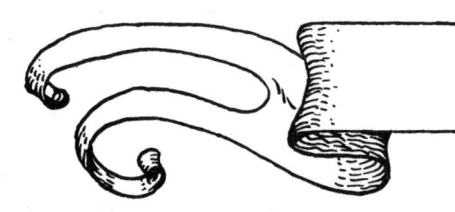

GRAVY

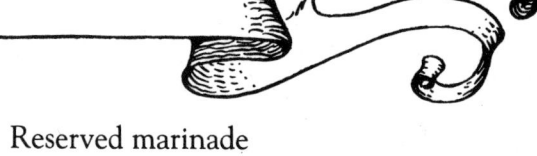

1 small onion, chopped
¼ cup dried Chilean mushrooms, chopped, or any dried mushrooms
Drippings from roasted duck

Reserved marinade
1 to 1½ tablespoons powdered chicken boullion

Sauté onions and mushroom in dripping over low heat. Add the marinade, more drippings, and boullion. Cook gently over medium heat until the gravy is slightly thickened.

Serve with Drunken Duck and wild rice.

The Amazons cook mainly outdoors on stoves, in clay ovens, and on spits. The kitchens inside their houses are used only for special convenience or during inclement weather.

Whenever the wizard Alzar comes to visit Sizaeo, he enjoys watching these regal women prepare meals. No effort is spared. The women entertain with great style. In return, Alzar rolls out the red carpet for them when they visit his mountaintop home. The wizard is particularly fond of barbecues, and naturally the women indulge their favorite guest.

Although the directions for the following recipe are given using an oven, it can be adapted to an outdoor grill. Make sure coals are not too hot, or the sauce will burn and lose its flavor.

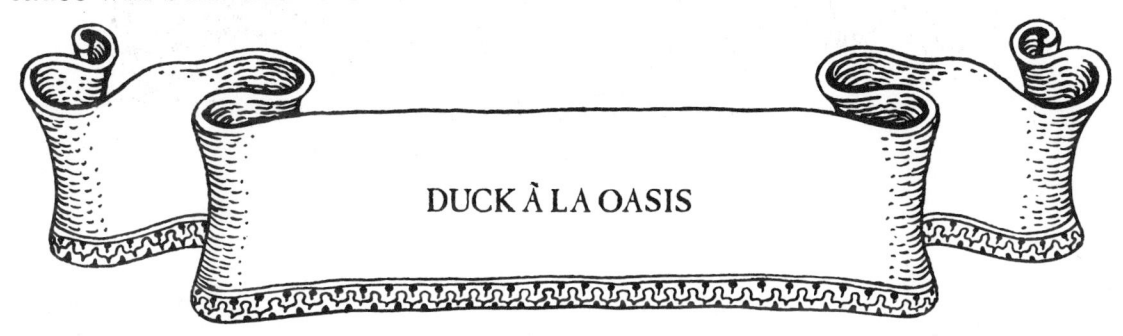

DUCK À LA OASIS

1 duck
1 cup dried turkish apricots
(They are hard and leathery, but the flavor is exquisite.)
Water
2 to 3 teaspoons red-currant or plum jam
3 to 4 tablespoons honey
¼ teaspoon onion powder
¼ teaspoon poultry seasoning
½ teaspoon rosemary

Preheat the oven to 375°.

Rinse the duck, clean it, and pat it dry. Place the duck in a pan and roast in the oven for 10 minutes while preparing the sauce.

To make the sauce, place the apricots in a saucepan with enough water to cover them, and bring to a boil. Simmer for 4 to 5 minutes. Reserve the apricot liquid and puree the apricots in a blender or food mill. Add enough of the hot apricot liquid to the pureed apricots to make a thick sauce. Mix into the sauce the jam, honey, onion powder, poultry seasoning, and rosemary.

Baste the duck with the sauce and roast it for 20 to 25 minutes per pound. When ready to serve, pass the sauce in a gravy boat.

Serves one Amazon if not very hungry, or 2 to 4 humans.

The Amazons created the following recipe in order to use leftover Duck Sauce à la Oasis. They serve this dish on a bed of cooked rice or millet surrounded by fresh fruit such as apricots, bananas, or crisp apples. A large green salad completes the meal.

Sauced Chicken

2 - 2½ to 3-pound fryers cut into serving pieces.
1 cup Amazon duck sauce (from previous recipe)
1 cup catsup
½ cup chili sauce
1 tablespoon mustard (yellow or Dijon type)
1 medium onion, chopped fine
½ teaspoon bouquet garni or Italian spice
½ bottle beer (6 ounces)

Cut chicken into serving pieces and pat dry. Toss lightly in some seasoned flour, and place in 350° oven, and roast for 5 minutes.

To prepare the sauce, combine all other ingredients in a bowl.

Baste the chicken with half the sauce, turning the pieces often. Continue to baste until the chicken is done, about 45 to 50 minutes.

Heat the remaining sauce and serve it with the chicken. The sauce can also be used with spareribs.

Serves 4 small Amazons or 6 humans.

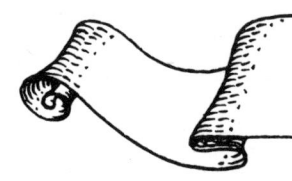

DUCK SALAD

1 cup cooked duck or dark turkey meat
1 cup cooked rice (wild, if possible)
4 dried or canned apricots, chopped
4 dates, pitted and chopped
½ cup chopped celery
Dressing (recipe follows)

Combine the above ingredients in a bowl and toss with dressing. Serve on lettuce leaves.

Serves 2 humans, or one Amazon for a snack.

Dressing

1 cup Mayonnaise
1 teaspoon curry powder
1-inch piece crystallized ginger, minced

Combine Mayonnaise, curry and ginger.

If there is any duck left from a meal the Amazons prepare a cold salad for the evening snack or the next day.

The Amazons use slight-of-hand tricks not only to develop dexterity but as entertainment at festivals. Naeomeena, one of the first high priestesses, developed a trick in which a kwee, a small magenta bird, would fly out of a sealed coconut when it was opened. She then would take an open, empty coconut and seal it closed. Naeomeena would call on a girl from the audience to tap the coconut and open it. Presto! The little bird would be inside! To honor this wonderful trick, Bird in a Coconut was invented.

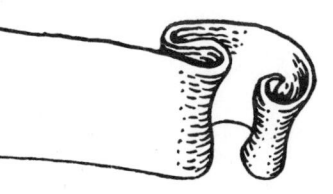

BIRD IN A COCONUT

4 coconuts in which to bake and serve chicken
2 large whole chicken breasts or 4 halves
Salt
1 teaspoon ground cumin
⅛ to ¼ teaspoon ground red pepper
1 teaspoon ground coriander seeds

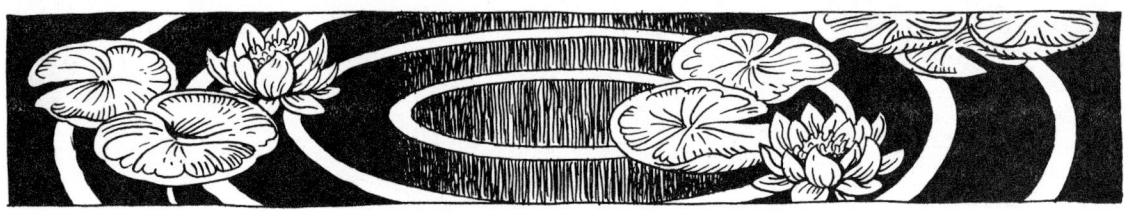

Flour for dredging
½ cup oil
½ cup finely chopped scallions
1½ teaspoon minced or crushed garlic
1 teaspoon turmeric
1 mashed banana
½ cup heavy cream
Milk from 1 coconut
1 egg, beaten

Preheat oven to 375°.

Puncture the eye of one coconut; drain out milk and reserve.

Split the coconuts in half by gently tapping lengthwise around the shell with a hammer. It will split almost perfectly. Remove the coconut meat from half of the shell and grate and toast it to use as garnish. Split the remaining coconuts. Set them aside.

Cut the chicken breasts in half, allowing half a breast per person. Salt and flour each piece and sauté it in the oil in a heavy skillet over medium heat, until it is golden brown and cooked through. Remove the chicken from the pan and keep it warm.

Add to the same oil the finely chopped scallions and minced garlic. Sauté until scallions are soft. Reduce the heat and add the turmeric, cumin, red pepper, coriander, mashed banana, cream, and milk from one coconut. Simmer for 3 to 5 minutes, then return chicken breasts to sauce.

Place one breast with some of the sauce in each of the shells lined with coconut meat. Cover with the other half of the shell and seal the crack all the way around with a dough made of the flour and water. Brush the dough with egg and bake until the dough is browned. The chicken will be warm.

To serve, crack off the top shell and serve the chicken in the bottom shell. Rice and broiled fruit, such as a combination of bananas, raisins, and pineapple, complete this unusual entree.

An alternative method is to heat the chicken in a covered casserole and serve it on a bed of rice topped with the broiled fruit. It will be less trouble and less expensive, but not as festive.

After serving, scoop out the meat from the coconut shells, wash them in hot water, and save them for the next time.

Serves 2 Amazons or 4 humans.

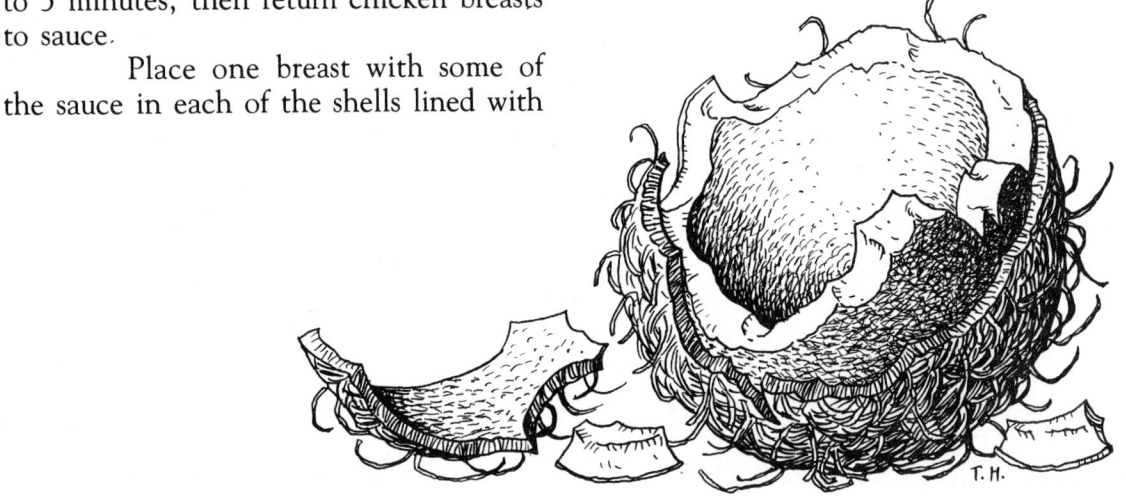

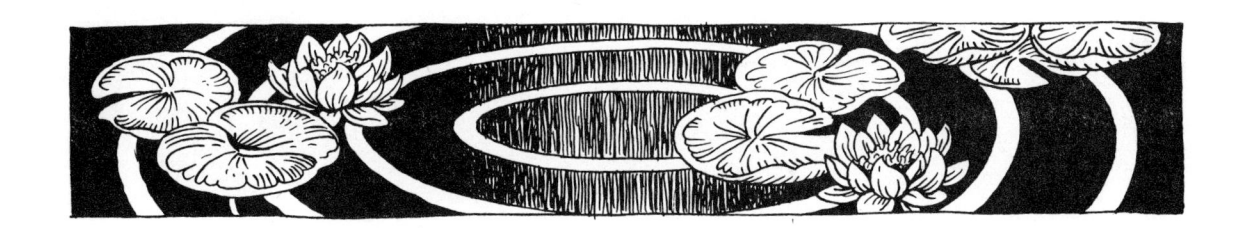

The Amazons love to invent and play elaborate games. Their games stress adventure or defense and can be played either on a board or be acted out by the players themselves, using costumes and appropriate settings. Winners receive prizes of beautifully designed costumes, sculptures, or even a version of a new game.

Game tournaments are only held every two years because of the time involved in preparing new games, embellishing old ones, and making the necessary costumes. The tournament lasts one week, during which the players are excused from field work or household chores. These games are taken very seriously and those not participating even make bets on the outcome.

Meals are light, because the excitement is high. During tournament time cooking and eating became secondary. Foods are either prepared in advance and served cold, or simple dishes are cooked quickly. The following recipe is popular during this intense time because it takes very little time and is hearty.

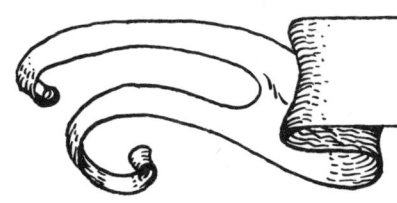

CHICKEN LIVERS

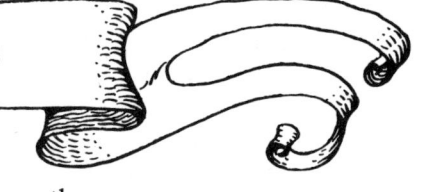

1 pound chicken livers
Flour, seasoned with salt and pepper
1½ to 2½ tablespoons melted butter
1 tablespoon oil
1 cup port wine
1 cup sliced mushrooms
Salt
Pepper

Roll the chicken livers in the seasoned flour. Sauté them in butter and oil until they are brown.

Remove the livers from pan and add another tablespoon of butter, if needed, to sauté the sliced mushrooms.

Add the chicken livers and port. Bring the liquid to a simmer. The flour on the chicken livers will make its own gravy. Add salt and pepper to taste.

Serve the livers and gravy immediately over rice, noodles, or whole-wheat-toast points.

Serves 2 Amazons or 4 humans.

Another meal served during the tournament features these spring morsels.

LAMB BALLS

¾ pound ground lamb
⅛ cup sesame seeds
⅓ cup All-Bran cereal
½ teaspoon curry powder
¼ teaspoon paprika
⅛ teaspoon ground cumin
2 cloves garlic, minced or crushed
½ teaspoon onion powder
1 teaspoon salt
½ cup yogurt

Mix the ground lamb with all the ingredients except the yogurt and form the mixture into one-inch balls.

Brown the lamb balls in 1½ teaspoons vegetable oil. Deglaze the pan when all the meatballs are brown.

Deglaze pan by adding the yogurt and heat thoroughly, but do not bring to a boil. Scrape any brown bits from the bottom of the pan.

Serve the lamb balls over saffron rice and noodles and top with yogurt sauce.

Serves one Amazon or 3 humans.

Many spices are available to the women, and they grind exotic combinations to produce currylike blends. These freshly ground spices should be used as quickly as possible. As with any ground spice or spice blend, the flavor fades with time. Storing them in the refrigerator preserves them longer. Here is one combination the Amazons especially like.

"CURRY," OR MIXED SPICE

1 1-inch-square piece of fresh ginger
10 whole cardamom pods
10 whole cloves
4 2-inch pieces of cinnamon stick
1 teaspoon cumin seeds
1 teaspoon ground turmeric
1 or 2 teaspoons ground red chile pods
4 medium bay leaves
2½ tablespoons dried spearmint
2½ teaspoons whole black peppercorns
3 teaspoons poppy seeds
2¼ teaspoons mustard seeds
2 teaspoons coriander seeds

Powder thoroughly in blender and store in a tightly sealed container.

Makes about ½ cup.

On hot days in the oasis the Amazons serve a "cool something" before meals. Sometimes it takes the form of a cold fruit soup or a drink, but most often it is a cold vegetable dip. Here is a favorite.

VEGETABLE DIP

4 cups chopped eggplant
½ cup chopped mushrooms
½ cup chopped onions
1 teaspoon curry powder
¼ cup yogurt
1 teaspoon butter
½ teaspoon Vegesal or salt

Prepare the vegetables and steam them in a covered saucepan until they are very soft. Mash with fork or vegetable masher. Stir in the remaining ingredients and refrigerate the dip until it is cold. It is best when made a day ahead. Serve with whole-wheat crackers, rye crackers, or on dark bread.

Serves 2 Amazons or 4 to 8 humans.

The ways of the strange women of Sizaeo seem mysterious to humans. Their life is monastic in many ways, but without stringent rules and regulations. The Amazons strive for physical and intellectual perfection. The spring in their oasis provides them with many extraordinary qualities and at the same time enhances each woman's particular traits and talents.

Among the talents the Amazons develop to great heights is their musical ability. Their haunting music is played on exquisitely made instruments. Anyone hearing their curious melodies falls into a peaceful trance, though only temporarily. This magic is said to arise from the tones of their wind instruments made from the horn shed by the unicorn once every hundred years.

To honor this mysterious animal the women created this recipe.

CARROT-FILBERT RING À LA UNICORN

1 pound carrots, peeled and cut into small pieces
½ cup filberts or hazelnuts
2 tablespoons butter
2 tablespoons flour
½ cup hot milk
4 eggs, separated
½ teaspoon salt

Preheat the oven to 350°.

Cook the carrots in a small amount of water until they are barely tender. Mash them or put them into a food processor for 15 seconds. Set aside.

Blanch the nuts by parboiling them in water and removing the skins by rubbing the nuts in a towel. Grate them or grind them in a processor. Set aside. These two steps may be done ahead of time.

Make a roux with butter and flour: melt the butter over low heat, sprinkle in the flour and stir it with a whisk. Cook it for about 2 minutes or until the flour bubbles slightly. Do not let it burn. Add the hot milk gradually and stir with the whisk until the cream sauce is thickened, about 4 to 5 minutes.

Lower the heat and add some of the cream sauce to a bowl containing the egg yolks. Then mix all the egg yolks into the remaining sauce.

Add the carrots, nuts, and salt. Simmer for 2 minutes, then cool slightly.

Meanwhile, beat the egg whites until they are stiff but not dry. Fold the carrot mixture into the egg whites and pour mixture into a buttered and floured soufflé dish.

Bake in a pan of hot water for 50 to 60 minutes.

Serves 2 Amazons or 6 humans.

NOTE: To make a ring that is to be unmolded, use only 2 cups of the cooked, pureed carrots. Bake the soufflé in a ring-shaped mold. Unmold the ring and serve with cooked peas in the center, or sprinkle the ring with chopped fresh parsley.

From the desert oasis to the Valley of the Unicorn it is only a short day's trip by pegasus. The Amazons travel there frequently to get materials for their jewelry making and sculpting. They also pick the fruits, vegetables, and herbs that grow in the valley. The unicorn and pegases have great psychic powers because they feed on the tops of a certain plant growing along the valley's stream. The Amazons dig the roots and prepare this vegetable, which tastes very much like carrots. They developed another recipe inspired by the magical animal and its valley.

CARROTS UNICORN

1½ tablespoons butter or oil
2⅓ cups sliced carrots
¼ teaspoon mace or ½ teaspoon nutmeg
¼ teaspoon allspice
¼ teaspoon Vegesal or salt
4 tablespoons chopped or figs
⅓ cup pineapple chunks
½ cup unpeeled, chopped apple
⅛ cup toasted cashews

Lightly sauté the carrots in butter or oil for 3 to 4 minutes. Add the spices and salt. Cover and cook over low heat until carrots are crunchy, yet tender. When they are ready, add the fruit and nuts and just heat through.

Serves 2 Amazons or 5 to 6 humans.

Trading with the dwarfs has brought many new items to the Amazons. However, they do restrict the amount of trade because the women wish to remain secluded. One of the foods they prize highly is broccoli, and when it comes into season, the flying horses are sent more frequently to Verderoc. In return, the Amazons give the dwarfs exotic fruits.

The Amazons prepare broccoli in many original ways. Here is one version that is very popular with the women.

BROCCOLI CASSEROLE

1 bunch broccoli
⅔ cup mayonnaise
9 tablespoons grated Romano or Parmesan cheese
½ to ⅔ cups sautéed almonds

Wash the broccoli and cut it lengthwise into sections. Steam it lightly until it turns bright green in color.

Mix the mayonnaise and cheese together. Place broccoli in an ovenproof casserole, top it with the mayonnaise-cheese mixture, and sprinkle the top with almonds. Broil until the cheese topping is lightly brown.

Serves 2 Amazons or 4 humans.

NOTE: Any leftover vegetables can be substituted for the broccoli, and any other nut or seed can replace the almonds. Sunflower seeds and cashews are particularly delicious.

The women of Sizaeo eat raw fruits and vegetables as an important part of their diet. They always have a salad with their meals. Most of the time it is simply a mixture of greens dressed with oil, citrus juices, and herbs. They also make different vinegars, using fruit juice or leftover wine in combination with herbs and spices. When they get broccoli from the dwarfs, this is one of their favorite salads.

AMAZON SALAD

1 bunch of broccoli
⅓ cup pitted black olives
6 radishes, sliced
¼ pound fresh, small, whole mushrooms
½ cup oil
3¼ tablespoons apple cider vinegar
1 teaspoon salt or Vegesal
¼ teaspoon pepper
1 clove garlic, minced
Pinch of nutmeg
⅓ cup feta cheese, crumpled
2 tomatoes, each cut into eight pieces
3 tablespoons whole pine nuts or slivered almonds

Separate the broccoli into flowerets and cut only the very tender stems into pieces. Save the remaining stems for soup.

Place in a plastic bag or large bowl the broccoli flowerets, olives, sliced radishes, and small mushrooms.

To prepare the dressing, mix together the oil, vinegar, salt, pepper, dry mustard, garlic, and nutmeg. Pour it over the broccoli mixture. Marinate the vegetables in the refrigerator for at least 4 hours in a covered container or plastic bag, turning once or twice to ensure that all the vegetables are covered with the marinade.

When ready to serve, drain the vegetables and add the cheese, tomatoes, and nuts. Toss and serve cold.

Serves 3 to 4 Amazons or 6 people generously.

NOTE: Cauliflower can be substituted for broccoli, and carrots make a nice addition to the salad.

The next recipe is one used for the morning meal out in the fields. It is easily fixed and transported.

ZUCCHINI-LEEK PIE

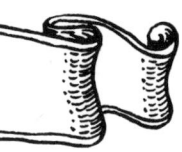

Crust

3 cups flour
4½ teaspoons baking powder
½ teaspoon soda
1 teaspoon salt
5 tablespoons butter
1 cup yogurt
Filling (recipe follows)

Preheat the oven to 450°.

Mix the flour, baking powder, soda, and salt together. Cut in butter until the mixture resembles coarse meal. Mix in the yogurt and press the dough into a 10-inch pie pan. Bake for 15 minutes at 450° until the crust is light tan in color.

This pie may be reheated successfully. For a thinner crust, use a regular pastry recipe.

Serves 3 Amazons or 8 humans.

Filling

2 cups of leek, thinly sliced in rounds (about 2 leeks)
4 cups zucchini, thinly sliced (about 2 medium)
3 to 4 tablespoons butter
¾ teaspoon salt
¼ teaspoon freshly ground pepper
2½ cups grated Muenster cheese

Wash and slice zucchini and leek. In a large pan melt the butter and sauté the leeks until they are soft. Add the zucchini, salt, and pepper, and cook for 10 minutes. Stir the cheese into the vegetables, pour into crust, and bake five minutes more at 450°.

The first snack eaten after rising almost always includes this delicious cream-cheese and jelly-filled pastry.

MORNING TURNOVER

1 recipe Troll's Bread (page 132)
1 3-ounce package cream cheese, divided into 8 slices
8 tablespoons guava, quince, papaya, mango, or other fruit jelly or jam
Oil for frying

Prepare the pastry dough. Divide the dough into 8 parts. Roll out each part into a 3- to 4-inch circle.

Place a slice of cream cheese and one tablespoon of jelly to one side of the circle. Fold over the dough and press the edges together, sealing them with a fork. Fry the turnovers in hot oil until golden brown. Serve immediately.

Makes 8 turnovers, to serve 2 Amazons or 8 humans.

When the dwarf child arrived in Sizaeo, the Amazons were competing in a racing and jumping tournament. After the excitement caused by his appearance died down, the games were finally completed.

The Amazons fed the child many exotic foods. He liked the curry buns best and he carried them back to Verderoc on his return, along with other gifts of food.

STEAMED CURRY BUNS

½ cup butter
⅓ cup turbinado sugar
2 teaspoons salt
¾ cup milk
2 packages yeast
½ cup warm water
1 teaspoon sugar
1 egg
4 cups flour
Waxed paper cut into 2-inch squares
Filling (recipe follows)

Melt the butter with ⅓ cup sugar, salt, and milk in a pan, then cool.

Proof the yeast in ½ cup warm water with 1 teaspoon sugar until the yeast is frothy.

Add the milk-butter mixture and the egg to the flour, and beat hard. Add the yeast. Knead until the dough does not stick to your hands.

Place the dough in a greased bowl and allow it to rise to double its bulk for about one hour or place it in the refrigerator overnight. Punch it down and form it into balls.

With your hands, spread the dough into rounds and fill each circle with the meat filling. Pull the dough around the meat so that it forms a bun shape. Place a piece of waxed paper on the bottom of each bun.

Steam buns in a steamer for 15 minutes. Wrap a towel around the lid of the steamer to prevent water drops from dripping on the buns as they steam.

Makes 12 large buns.

Filling

1 medium onion, minced
1 clove garlic, minced
2 teaspoons oil
1 pound of lamb or beef
1 tablespoon cornstarch
2 tablespoons soy sauce
1 tablespoon curry powder

In a skillet sauté the onions and garlic in the oil until they are soft.

Mix the meat, cornstarch, and soy sauce together and add the mixture to the onions. Brown meat. Add the curry powder and cook a minute or two longer.

This filling can also be used in piecrust turnovers.

In their outdoor clay ovens the Amazons bake wonderful breads, and no meal or snack is complete without some type of bread. The yeast-bread recipe that follows is used in many variations. It can be prepared as a loaf with nuts or swirls of spices and honey or of course can be made into rolls, as in this version.

ROLLS À LA SIZAEO

1 cake yeast or 1 package dry yeast
1¼ cup water
1 teaspoon sugar
3½ to 4 cups flour
1 teaspoon salt
¼ cup turbinado sugar or honey
¼ teaspoon ground cardamon
2 tablespoons butter or oil
1 beaten egg, at room temperature
Melted butter

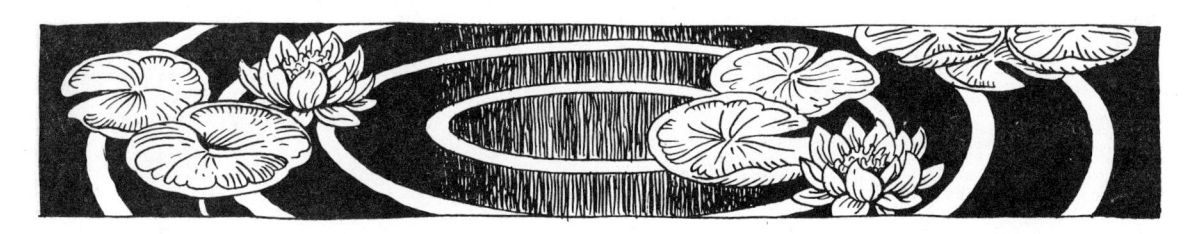

Proof the yeast in ¼ cup warm water with 1 teaspoon sugar.

Mix together 2 cups of the flour, salt, sugar or honey, cardamon, butter, and 1 cup water. Beat hard until gluten is formed and the batter is stringy. Add the yeast mixture and remaining flour.

Knead until the dough is no longer sticky. Let it rise until it doubles in bulk.

Punch it down and add the egg. Knead again and let rise again until it is nearly double in size.

Preheat the oven to 375°.

Punch down the dough and form it into 1½-inch balls. With a rolling pin roll each ball into a 3-inch round. Spread each round with melted butter and fold over.

Place the rolls in greased muffin tins or line them up in a shallow baking pan. Bake them for 25 to 30 minutes if using muffin tins, or approximately 40 minutes if using a baking pan.

Makes 24 rolls, enough for 6 Amazons.

Here is another wonderful recipe the Amazons prepare in their clay ovens.

MUFFINS À LA AMAZONS

¼ pound butter
1¼ cup raw sugar
½ teaspoon sea salt
4 eggs
1½ cups yogurt

2¾ cups unbleached flour
1 teaspoon baking soda
⅛ to ¼ teaspoon nutmeg, freshly grated

Preheat the oven to 450°.

In a bowl beat together the butter, sugar, and salt until light.

In a separate bowl beat the eggs until they are thick and lemon-colored. Add the eggs to the butter-sugar mixture. Beat for one to 2 minutes more. Add the yogurt.

In a clean bowl mix together the flour, soda, and nutmeg. Add the flour to the egg-butter mixture. Mix just until blended.

Spoon the butter into muffin tins. Bake for 15 minutes.

Makes 16 medium muffins, enough to serve 4 Amazons.

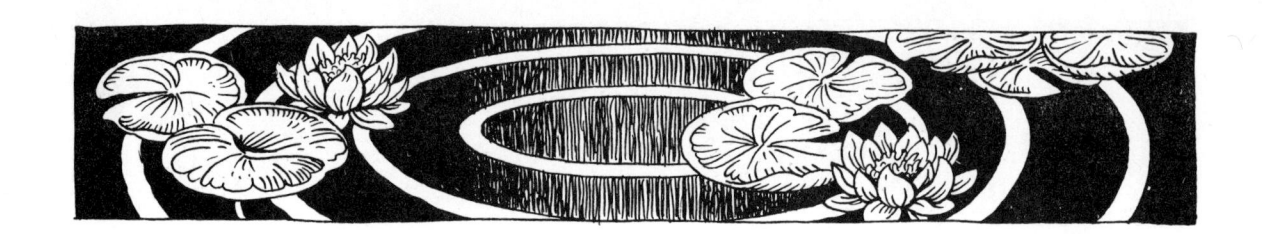

Alzar the wizard was a young man when he first visited Sizaeo, and he caused quite a stir in the oasis. The Amazons realized almost immediately that he was a friend and aide. During his short stay, Alzar taught them how to control their newfound mental powers, and even though he was a youth, he gave them advice about the outside world and their life in the oasis.

During this visit, Alzar also experienced something new. It was his first taste of Banana Puff. He liked it with custard sauce poured on top, although the Amazons prefer to eat it plain.

BANANA PUFF

4 very ripe bananas
2 eggs, separated
2 tablespoons melted butter
½ cup sour cream
1 tablespoon lemon juice
Rind of ½ lemon or ¼ teaspoon dried peel
¼ cup brown sugar or maple syrup
Allspice
Meringue (recipe follows)

Preheat the oven to 400°.

Run the bananas through a food processor or ricer or mash them with a masher.

If using a processor, place the egg yolks, melted butter, sour cream, lemon juice, and lemon rind in the processor and process for about 30 seconds. If not using a processor, beat the egg yolks until they are lemon-colored and add bananas, melted butter, sour cream, lemon juice, and lemon rind to the egg yolks.

Beat the egg whites until almost stiff. Add ¼ cup of maple syrup or brown sugar. Beat until the whites are stiff but not dry. Fold the banana-egg yolk mixture into the beaten egg whites.

Pour the mixture into custard cups or ramekins that have been buttered and dusted with allspice. Set cups in a baking pan and pour in enough hot water to reach halfway up cups' sides. Bake for

15 minutes.

Remove the ramekins from the oven and top them with the meringue. Bake 10 to 15 minutes, until the meringue is brown. Serve warm or ice cold.

Makes 6 ½-cup servings, enough for 2 Amazons.

Meringue

2 egg whites
Pinch of cream of tartar
Pinch of salt
5 tablespoons brown sugar or maple syrup

While the banana mixture is cooking, make the meringue. Beat the 2 egg whites until they are foamy. Add the cream of tartar and salt. Beat until almost stiff. Add the brown sugar while continuing to beat.

With the sun as an ally, the women of Sizaeo dry many of their foods. They also rely on their spring for refrigeration; thus, food storage is simplified. Here is a recipe using dried fruits.

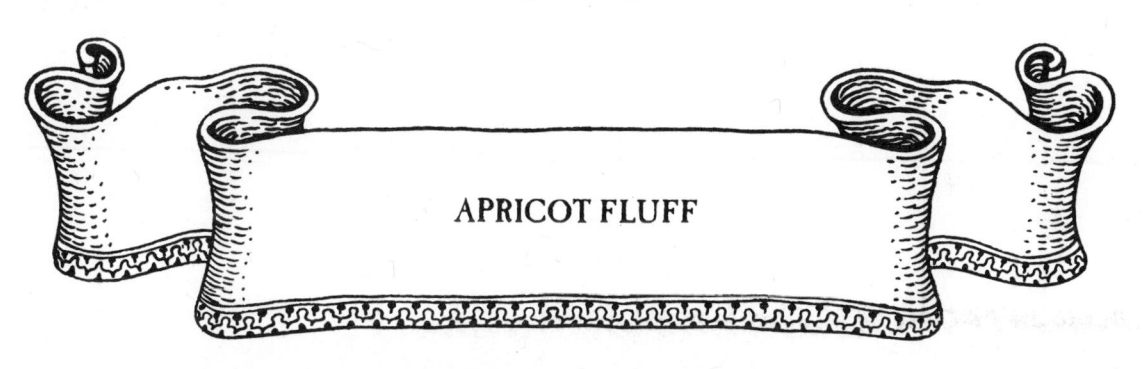

APRICOT FLUFF

⅛ cup honey
1 cup dried apricots, stewed and pureed
3 egg whites
1 teaspoon lemon juice
Pinch of salt

Preheat the oven to 300°.
Combine the honey and the stewed, pureed apricots. Set aside.
Beat the egg whites until they are foamy. Add the lemon juice and salt. Continue beating until the whites are stiff.
Fold the egg whites into apricot-honey mixture. Pile the mixture into a greased one-quart mold.
Bake for 35 minutes.
Serve at once with custard sauce, zabaglione, or softened, beaten ice cream.

Serves 4.

Because they have such long life spans, the Amazons do not have birthday parties. Naturally records are kept of their ages, but since they have almost eternal youth, strength, and beauty, they don't bother to celebrate each year.

What comes closest to an anniversary party are the feasts given by each high priestess during her tenure in office. The celebrations are lavish events during which gifts are given to the priestess, and there are songs and dances. Time is set aside for each woman to air her complaints if she has any, or to laud the ruler, which is usually the case. At these celebrations the high priestess chooses a menu of her favorite dishes, which are then prepared by the council and its committee.

Here's one of the High Priestess Dila's favorite dishes.

MANGO MOUSSE

2 packets unflavored gelatin
2 tablespoons cold water
¼ cup boiling water
1 tablespoon lime juice
2 cups canned mango, pureed and chilled
2 cups heavy cream, whipped

Soften the gelatin in the cold water. Add boiling water to the softened gelatin and stir until it is completely dissolved.

Mix the lime juice into the pureed mango.

Stir the pureed mango into the gelatin, then fold the whipped cream into the gelatin mixture.

Pour into a soufflé dish and chill until set.

If the mango puree is slightly frozen before starting, the mixture will harden sooner.

Serves one Amazon or 6 to 8 humans.

Culinary skills are considered an art in Sizaeo. Everyone learns to cook. As in any society, however, some women are more skilled than others. Twice yearly a culinary fair is arranged and prizes are given for the best dishes in many categories. Younger women generally exhibit more enthusiasm for the event, but occasionally the council will arranged a competition for the older women only. They have great fun preparing their entries, as well as eating them. This recipe was a winner in the dessert category.

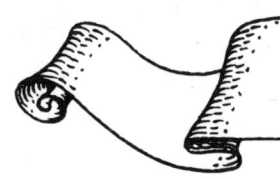

TANGERINE SHORTCAKE

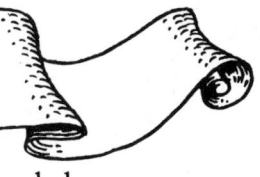

¼ to ½ cup orange blossom honey
2 tablespoons butter
2 tablespoons cornstarch
½ teaspoon grated tangerine rind or orange rind
⅓ cup tangerine juice or orange juice
2½ cups tangerines, seeded but not peeled
2 tablespoons Cointreau (optional)
Whipped cream sweetened with honey and flavored with vanilla
Pastry rounds (recipe follows)

Combine the honey, butter, cornstarch, and tangerine rind and juice, and cook over medium heat until the sauce is thick. Then cook for one minute more. Add the tangerines and the Cointreau, if desired.

To serve, place one pastry round on a plate. Cover it with ¼ cup tangerine sauce, top with another round and spoon more sauce over it. Garnish with whipped cream.

Serves 2 Amazons or 6 humans.

Pastry

1½ cups flour
½ teaspoon salt
½ cup oil
5 tablespoons milk
1½ teaspoons honey or sugar

Preheat the oven to 350°.

Combine the flour and salt. Then mix together the oil, milk, and honey, and add them to the flour.

Form the pastry into a ball and roll it out to ⅛-inch thickness. Cut it into 2½-inch rounds. Using a spatula, lift the rounds and place them on a lightly greased baking sheet.

Bake the pastries for 18 to 20 minutes. Cool them on wire racks and store in airtight container until ready to use.

Amazons eat many steamed cakes and breads, because their preparation produces little additional heat in their desert climate. The bread crumbs in this cake give it a light texture.

AMAZON BLACK CAKE

¼ cup butter
1 cup honey
2 eggs, separated
¾ teaspoon vanilla
1½ cup whole-wheat pastry flour or unbleached flour
1 cup fresh oatmeal bread crumbs (whole-wheat bread crumbs can be substituted)
2½ teaspoons baking powder
1 teaspoon cinnamon
½ teaspoon cloves or allspice
½ teaspoon nutmeg
½ cup cashews, chopped
¾ cup chopped dates (Medjool are the best)
1 cup heavy cream, or half-and-half
Golden Sauce (recipe follows)

Have ready a buttered mold or coffee can for steaming and a pan large enough to accommodate the mold and a small amount of water.

Cream the butter and honey together. Add the egg yolks and vanilla, beating until the mixture is fluffy and lemon-colored.

Mix together the flour, bread crumbs, baking powder, spices, nuts, and dates. Add the cream to the dry ingredients, then mix in the butter-egg mixture.

Beat the 2 egg whites and fold them into the cake batter.

Pour the batter into the mold. (If coffee can is used, cover with aluminum foil.) Set mold in pan and add enough boiling water to reach midway up mold. Steam the cake at a low boil for 1½ hours. Serve hot with Golden Sauce.

Serves 4 to 6 Amazons or 8 to 10 humans.

GOLDEN SAUCE

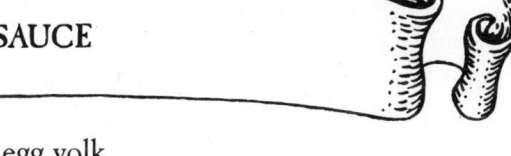

2½ tablespoons arrowroot or corn starch
1½ cups water
¾ cups honey
1 egg yolk
¼ teaspoon salt
⅓ cup lemon juice
3 teaspoons lemon peel

Mix all the ingredients in a saucepan with a wire whisk. Cook over low to medium heat until the sauce is thick. Serve warm or cold. This sauce may also be used over gingerbread, ice cream, or crepes, or over sponge cake with strawberries. It has a very lemony flavor.

An ever present mirage surrounding Sizaeo protects the women from intruders. To achieve this cover, the Amazons use a form of meditation that creates the mirage while at the same time enhancing their mental powers. Each woman must devote time to perfecting certain mental feats. To prepare herself for a period of psychic gymnastics, an Amazon drinks only fruit and vegetable juices. This diet has a calming effect and heightens her mental state.

The following drink was created by Pineena during her term in the council. It has become an all-time favorite.

AMAZON DRINK

3 cups papaya juice
1½ bananas
½ cup frozen unsweetened strawberries
2 to 4 tablespoons honey (optional)
2 ice cubes

Place all the ingredients into a blender and blend. The mixture will be thick and frosty.

VARIATION: One-half cup frozen raspberries may be used instead of strawberries.

Even in the extraordinary world of Zir, the Amazons are strange and mysterious. Secluded in their oasis, they seek the perfection of mind and body. With the gifts bestowed on them by the magical spring waters in their oasis, they seem to have achieved it.

ALZAR THE WIZARD

At the very end of the peninsula that juts out from the continent of Zir, Alzar, a young wizard, lives in a rambling stone house perched on a mountaintop overlooking the sea. How and when he arrived at Zir, Alzar keeps a mystery. Only the fairy queen, Aureena, knows, and his secret is safe with her. He lives alone except for his eccentric pet dragon, Draco Timate Nebulus Rex, whom he affectionately calls Neby. The dark-haired sorcerer welcomes guests freely, however, for he is still young by wizard standards, enjoys company, and readily gives his counsel to those who seek it.

As all wizards do, Alzar spends time practicing his crafts of alchemy, conjuring, and other kinds of magic. He also tends his herb and flower gardens, along with his fruit-filled orchards. His house surrounds a small volcanic pond that serves as home to many waterfowl which the sorcerer loves to observe. At the very edge of the mountain peak grows a large buttonwood tree. On the tree hangs an ornately carved chair in which Alzar swings out over the sea and views the breakers as they crash against the rocks that hug the base of his mountain.

As historian and chronicler of Zir, Alzar frequently visits all the peoples of Zir and closely observes their life-styles. Though he eagerly awaits invitations to festivals and celebrations, he will occasionally make surprise visits to bring gifts or offer his friends help when it is needed.

Guests who visit the wizard notice the serene atmosphere as they enter his house. Alzar is the perfect host and loves to entertain. Many of those who come hold him in awe, but he is eager to make them feel welcome. And everyone is happily greeted by Neby, Alzar's amazing red dragon, who acts more like a friendly collie than a flying reptile.

Entertaining usually takes the form of a tea party or light hors d'oeuvres similar to those served at a human cocktail party. Alzar never gives dinner parties as such, but when guests come, food is abundant. When there are no guests, the wizard and his dragon dine lightly on fruit, cheeses, and salads. Sometimes Neby will rummage in the garden for extra morsels, but generally he is content with what he is served. He and Alzar always eat together, even when the two are out visiting.

For his table Alzar chooses from all the foods available in Zir and even some that he creates himself. "Variety if not abundance" is his motto. He himself eats no red meat but prepares poultry and seafood. Many of his seafood dishes are of merpeople origin, so they are not included in this chapter. On occasion he drinks wine but prefers a variety of fruit drinks, especially those that are fizzy. He is particularly fond of the fairies' Celebration Sparkle. He also drinks vegetable juices, milk, and exotic combinations of herbal teas.

Alzar usually eats six, but sometimes ten or twelve, times a day. He starts the day with an egg-milk drink. He may have fruit for lunch or a small salad with oil, vinegar, and herbs. In the afternoon he will snack on cheese and crackers or bread with fruit juice. For dinner he prefers a fruit salad, and before bed he has vegetable juice and bread or perhaps just crackers with fruit jam and tea. He adores sweets, mainly in the form of pastries and cookies, but eats them sparingly and only when he entertains.

When Fairy Queen Aureena presented Alzar with Neby, her intention was that this gift would help the wizard increase his patience and curb his short temper. She gave Neby to Alzar on the occasion of his first Annual Light and Magic Show. Since then she has given him a gift every year, but none has been as wonderful or exasperating as the flying reptile. Neby is a special creature who is normally the size of a dog. But he has the ability to alter his size to suit the occasion. For example, to sit on Alzar's lap, Neby becomes cat-size, but if the wizard wants a ride to see the Amazons, Neby grows to the size of a large horse. Like a chameleon, the dragon alters his normally red color to suit the environment or mood. To communicate he uses telepathy. This lovable dragon is Alzar's companion, pet, and pest.

Neby hates being alone; he follows so closely at Alzar's heels that the wizard sometimes loses patience. If the dragon is locked out of the laboratory, he scratches frantically at the door, whining loudly. However, if Alzar lets him into the room while he is conjuring, Neby will jump up to play with the images the wizard creates or nibble at the secret ingredients in his experiments. Occasionally, though, Neby will be content to stay out of the way and only watch.

Before meals he rubs catlike against Alzar's legs as Alzar prepares the food, sometimes tripping him, which infuriates the wizard. Nonetheless, the two are very close, and whatever Alzar eats the dragon shares and considers a delicacy. One of Neby's favorites is Noodles à la Dragon.

NOODLES À LA DRAGON

8 ounces very thin spaghetti
2 small cloves garlic, minced or pressed
⅓ cup chopped onions or leeks
⅓ cup butter
2 cups sour cream
2 cups cottage cheese
1¼ teaspoon Worcestershire sauce
1 teaspoon salt
¼ teaspoon pepper
½ cup grated Parmesan cheese

Preheat the oven to 350°.

Cook the spaghetti in boiling water until it is *al dente*.

Sauté the garlic and onion in butter until they are translucent.

Mix together the sour cream, cottage cheese, Worcestershire sauce, salt, and pepper. Add the sautéed onions and garlic and the Parmesan cheese.

Turn the mixture into the cooked spaghetti and toss. Place in an ovenproof casserole and bake in the oven for 10 to 15 minutes to heat the pasta.

Serves 8 humans, one dragon named Neby, or 4 Amazons.

Contemplation and meditation are a regular part of Alzar's life. His only problem is friendly Neby, who wants his constant companionship. At first the wizard was not able to concentrate, because the dragon would sit quietly for only a short time and then, in a burst of enthusiasm, would give Alzar's face a lick with his hot tongue. Gone was the wizard's meditation. He started casting spells on the dragon to make him quiet, but that was very draining to Alzar. So now he hypnotizes Neby during the meditation hour, but this is the only time he does it. He seems to like the exuberant nature of his dragon.

After meditating, Alzar eats something light, and it usually takes the form of a soufflé. Here is his favorite Eggplant Soufflé.

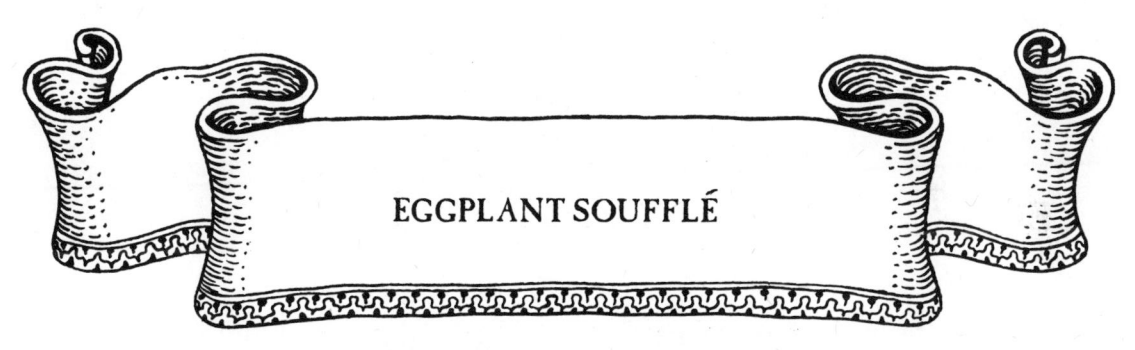

EGGPLANT SOUFFLÉ

2 large eggplants
½ to ⅓ cup chopped leeks or onions (preferably leeks)
½ cup water
5 tablespoons butter
6½ tablespoons flour
1 teaspoon salt
5 grinds nutmeg (or large pinch)
2 cups hot milk
8 eggs, separated

Preheat the oven to 350°.

Cut the eggplants lengthwise and scoop out their centers, leaving a shell ¼ inch thick. Chop the scooped-out eggplant and measure out 5 cups.

Place the chopped eggplant in a large skillet, add the leek or onion, and water and cook until tender. Measure out 2 cups of the cooked eggplant and puree it.

In a saucepan make a roux. Melt the butter on low heat, add flour, salt, and nutmeg and stir with a wire whisk. Cook until the flour bubbles slightly. Add the hot milk gradually, continuing to stir with a whisk. When the mixture is thick, add the 8 beaten egg yolks and cook for one to 2 minutes longer. Remove the egg and flour mixture from the heat and add the pureed eggplant.

Beat the egg whites until they are stiff but not dry. Fold them into the eggplant mixture. Pour the soufflé mixture into the eggplant shells and bake them in an ovenproof dish for 35 to 40 minutes. Serve at once.

Serves 4 to 6 humans.

Alzar is most at peace when working in his gardens. He loves to make things grow without the use of magic. However, he is sometimes tempted to help nature out when things are not going just right. Human gardeners have their frustrations, and on rare occasions even Alzar is faced with a withered leaf. But his home is a jungle of flourishing plants. The only two rooms bare of leafy things are his laboratory and his bed chamber. Even Neby has his own plant, similar to catnip, only it is dragonnip.

Because he is such an avid gardener, Alzar has lots of produce, which he mainly eats raw but sometimes steams or bakes. The following is a tasty vegetable casserole he originally created for a visitor.

VISITOR'S CASSEROLE

3 cups fresh vegetables in bite-size pieces (any combination of celery, green beans, lima beans, or summer squash)
⅓ cup toasted slivered almonds
½ cup water chestnuts
3 tablespoons butter
3 tablespoons flour

1 cup chicken or vegetable broth
¾ cup light cream or half-and-half
½ cup mushrooms, sliced
½ cup Parmesan cheese, grated
½ cup cereal crumbs (shredded wheat, corn flakes, or Grape Nuts)
2 tablespoons butter

Preheat the oven to 350°.

Place the vegetables, almonds, and water chestnuts in an ovenproof casserole.

In a saucepan make a roux with 3 tablespoons of melted butter and the flour. Add the broth and cream to the roux, stirring constantly. Cook until the sauce is thick. Add the mushrooms. Pour the sauce over the vegetable mixture.

Cover the casserole with the grated cheese and then the cereal crumbs. Dot with 2 tablespoons butter.

Bake until bubbly, about 15 to 20 minutes.

Serves 10 to 12 elves, or 2 Amazons, or 6 humans, or one wizard and his dragon.

Once Alzar conjured up a dish for some dwarfs who came to visit very unexpectedly on an important matter. Naturally the dwarfs, who love to cook as well as eat, asked for the recipe. Alzar gave them the following recipe. When the dwarfs tried it out, they informed the wizard that he had given them the wrong recipe but that they liked this one just as well!

THE WRONG RECIPE

¾ pounds ground lamb
¼ cup sesame seeds
⅓ cup All-Bran
1 clove garlic, minced
½ teaspoon rosemary
⅛ teaspoon celery seed
⅛ teaspoon thyme
9 turns of the pepper grinder, or pepper to taste
1 teaspoon salt
1 tablespoon oil
¼ cup water
¼ to ½ cup vermouth

Mix the lamb, sesame seeds, All-Bran, garlic, ¼ cup water, herbs, salt, and pepper together and form the mixture into one-inch balls. Sauté the balls in the oil until browned. Add the vermouth and bring mixture to a boil for 2 or 3 minutes to evaporate the alcohol. Add the water, cover, and steam for 5 to 10 minutes more. The lamb balls can be kept hot or reheated successfully. Serve them over rice, cous-cous, or as hot hors d'oeuvres.

Serves 3 to 4 humans as a meal, or 6 guests at the wizard's house for appetizers.

When the Amazons or dwarfs come to Alzar's mountain he prepares larger meals. But even these meals are small compared to what his guests normally eat at home. Somehow, though, they are never hungry. This satisfied feeling even lasts for a day or two after they leave the magician's home.

When he brings gifts of food to his hosts, a little goes a long way, and that says a lot when the amounts consumed by dwarfs and giants are considered.

Here is the Amazons' favorite dish when they dine at Alzar's.

BIRD IN CRUST

1 3-pound whole chicken and giblets
4 green onions, chopped fine
2 tablespoons butter
6 to 8 slices whole-wheat bread, cubed or diced
¼ cup broth or milk
2 teaspoons minced parsley
¼ teaspoon thyme
¼ teaspoon salt, or to taste
3 to 4 slices of bacon, chopped and cooked

1 beaten egg
2 tablespoons calvados

Crust (recipe follows)

Make a broth by simmering the neck, gizzard, heart, and liver in 1½ cups water for about an hour. After cooking the broth, reserve the liver and chop it finely.

Prepare the crust.

Preheat the oven to 375°.

Wash the chicken and dry it thoroughly.

To make the stuffing, sauté the green onions in the butter. In a bowl mix the bread cubes and broth, then add the green onion, parsley, thyme, salt, chopped chicken liver, and chopped, cooked bacon. Beat the egg with brandy and add. Stuff the bird and truss it (pin or sew the cavity's opening and tie the drumsticks together).

Roll out the dough to ¼-inch thickness, until it is large enough to cover the bird. Place the chicken on its side on the pastry and seal the dough along the backbone. Cut out leaf and flower shapes and decorate the dough-covered chicken in a pleasing manner. Poke steam holes in the crust along the two thighs. Use the egg wash over the entire crust; it will brown beautifully.

Place the chicken in a pan for 1½ to two hours. Check the internal temperature by placing a meat thermometer through one of the steam holes and into the thigh. The chicken is done when the thermometer registers 190°.

Serves one Amazon, or one dragon and one wizard, or 4 humans.

Crust

1½ cups flour
¼ teaspoon salt
½ cup butter

1 egg beaten with 1 tablespoon of water for egg wash

Combine the ingredients in the order given and mix with hand until a ball of dough is formed. Let the dough rest for 10 minutes.

Curry Buns are usually served to the Amazons when they come to visit. They love any food made with curry or spices. Alzar will sometimes eat a curry bun hot from the oven for his morning snack.

CURRY BUNS

6 tablespoons butter
½ cup brown or turbinado sugar
1 egg

½ teaspoon curry powder or ¼ teaspoon cumin plus
¼ teaspoon turmeric

1½ cups flour (¾ cup unbleached and ¾ cup whole-wheat)
¾ teaspoon salt
1½ teaspoon baking powder
Filling (recipe follows)

Preheat the oven to 375°.

Beat the butter and sugar together. Add the egg and curry powder.

Mix together the flour, salt, and baking powder and add them to the butter-egg mixture.

Spoon into greased and floured muffin tins, filling the cups only ¼ full, then adding ½ tablespoon of filling and topping with more batter. Sprinkle the tops with extra brown sugar. Bake for 20 minutes.

Makes about 12 buns.

Serves 3 visiting Amazons or one hungry dragon.

Filling

½ cup unsweetened apple sauce
3 tablespoons brown or turbinado sugar

Mix together applesauce and sugar.

On days when Alzar is alone or does not feel like traveling, he will, weather permitting, pack a lunch and stroll out to his swing. The carved chair is hung from a limb far out over the edge of the mountain. Climbing along the limb of the great buttonwood tree, he eases himself onto the seat and swings for a long while, then lets the chair come to a stop. There, dangling out over the breakers, he watches the world below. He envisions the past, present, and future of Zir. While immersed in his visions he may be startled by a wet, hot tongue lapping at his face — Neby.

After a very slight reprimand to his flying nuisance (for Alzar knows full well his companion loves to swing), the wizard will offer lunch to the dragon. There will be spiced muffins with butter or cheese, some fruit, and perhaps leftover fish or chicken from the day before. Certainly something to drink will be included. After they have eaten there is more swinging. Strangely enough, the dragon sits calmly on the sorcerer's lap as they glide back and forth through the air.

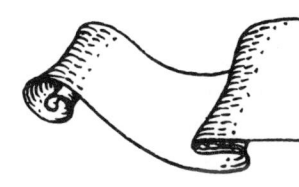

SPICED MUFFINS

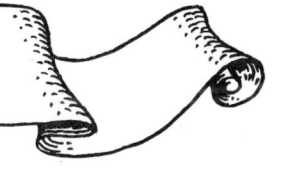

1½ cups flour
½ cup wheat germ
1 tablespoon allspice
½ tablespoon cloves
⅛ teaspoon salt
¾ cup brown or turbinado sugar
1 cup yogurt
½ cup butter, melted
2 eggs, beaten
½ cup chopped nuts

Preheat the oven to 425°.

In a bowl mix all the dry ingredients together.

Beat together the eggs and yogurt along with the melted butter. Add to the dry ingredients. Do not overbeat. Some of flour mixture will still be dry.

Spoon the batter into greased and floured muffin tins. Bake for 20 to 25 minutes.

Makes 12, enough for one dragon and one wizard.

Long ago, when the elf prince, Timmekin, asked Alzar to help rid their land of the great black beast that was threatening to destroy the elfin city, the sorcerer came to the rescue. Since that time the elfs have in gratitude prepared a feast for the Annual Light and Magic Show. After the wizard gives his light and fireworks show, those who attend enjoy the elfin festival. The elfs handle the whole feast, cooking, waiting on tables, and cleaning up. Every year the food is different, but it is always delicious.

Here are two appetizer recipes from one of the banquets.

The following recipe was originally made with a long white vegetable called kiku, which is thinly sliced lengthwise and smoked in the large elfin ovens. To duplicate the taste, naturally smoked bacon has been substituted. Use the kind that has no added chemicals. It can be purchased in natural-food stores.

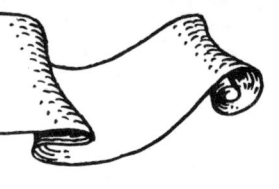

SPICY ROLL-UPS

1 pound bacon slices
1 can water chestnuts
1 can shrimp, or ½ pound peeled and cleaned shrimp
¾ cup chili sauce
1 tablespoon tamari or soy sauce
1 teaspoon brown sugar or molasses

Preheat oven to 375°.
Cut strips of bacon into thirds. Roll one water chestnut in a piece of bacon; use a toothpick to secure the bacon on the water chestnut.
Prepare the shrimp in the same manner. If canned shrimp is used, ½ teaspoon of shrimp should be wrapped in the ⅓ piece of bacon.
Make a sauce by mixing together the chili sauce, tamari, and molasses.

When all the bacon has been used, place the roll-ups on a broiling pan and brush them with the sauce, using a pastry brush.
Broil the roll-ups for 5 minutes, then turn and brush with more sauce. Broil again until nicely browned. Served immediately.

Serves 6 humans, or one dragon, or one or 2 dwarfs.

Here is another favorite from the feast.

APPETIZER ROLLS

2 cups flour
1 teaspoon salt
1½ teaspoons dried mustard
½ teaspoon garlic powder
Pinch to ⅛ teaspoon cayenne pepper
⅔ cup butter
5 to 6 tablespoons water
Fillings (recipe follows)

Preheat oven to 400°.
Mix the flour, salt, dried mustard, garlic powder, and cayenne pepper together in bowl. Cut in the butter as if for a pie crust and add the water.
Mix together to form a dough. Chill the dough in the refrigerator for 2 hours or overnight.

Divide dough in 4 equal portions and roll in out in rectangles, leaving dough about ¼ inch thick. It is much easier to roll the dough when you do it between layers of waxed paper.
Spread 2 rectangles with the cheddar cheese and chutney filling and 2 with the Parmesan cheese and anchovy

mixture. Roll each rectangle into a jelly-roll shape and chill for 2 hours or more.

When you are ready to serve them, slice the rolls in ¼-inch slices and bake at 400° for 12 to 14 minutes.

Makes three dozen cheddar-chutney and 3 dozen anchovy-Parmesan rolls.

Serves one dragon and one wizard during an afternoon of playing board games, or 2 Amazons for snacks in the evening.

Fillings

Filling I

¾ cup of cheddar cheese
2 to 4 tablespoons chutney

Filling II

4 to 6 anchovies fillets
½ cup grated Parmesan cheese

Filling III

Minced chicken
Mayonnaise

For this version mix ½ teaspoon ginger into the pastry dough.

On rainy afternoons Alzar occasionally plays games, usually a board game something like chess, only with more pieces and slightly different rules. The dragon has some intelligence and is usually his opponent. Mind you, it is really not a fair game. Usually Alzar lets Neby win. It makes the reptile buoyant.

They snack and play for hours, the dragon doing most of the snacking on this tasty treat.

CHEESE AND CRUST

Brie or Camembert cheese
Very good dry white wine
⅓ cup sweet butter for every cup of cheese
Fine, toasted bread crumbs or chopped nuts

Use any amount of cheese and cut off the skin.

Place the cheese in a glass or ceramic bowl and add enough wine to cover. Let the cheese stand in the refrigerator for at least 12 hours, but not more than 2 days.

Remove the cheese from the wine and beat the butter and cheese together with a mixer, processor, or by hand.

Shape the mixture into a round or oval shape and roll it in toasted, fine bread crumbs or chopped nuts.

Use Cheese and Crust as a first course or hors d'oeuvre. Serve with crackers, bread sticks, or crudités.

Serves one dragon and one wizard on a rainy afternoon, or 4 to 6 humans.

Now and again the mountain vibrates with the sound of music emanating from the rambling stone house. Alzar plays many instruments to entertain himself and Neby when they are alone. Sometimes, he "invites"

the other instruments to join him in making a quartet or even an orchestra of sorts.

All who visit with Alzar love music, and most of them play instruments or sing. Alzar's jam sessions, held either alone or with guests, are happy times for all.

After one of these gatherings, Alzar usually serves a mixed vegetable salad, cheese pie, crackers or rolls, fruit for dessert, and perhaps a cake. Music makes him hungry.

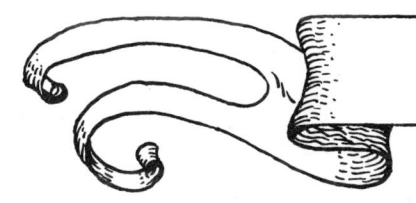

CHEESE PIE

2 cups heavy cream or 1 cup milk and 1 cup cream
4 eggs
½ teaspoon salt
½ cup Swiss cheese, grated
⅛ teaspoon white pepper
1 to 2 tablespoons Parmesan cheese, grated
Pinch of nutmeg
1 9-inch pie shell, unbaked (page 21)

Preheat the oven to 425°

In a bowl beat the eggs. Add the cream, salt, white pepper, and nutmeg. Add the Swiss and Parmesan cheeses and mix thoroughly. Pour the mixture into an unbaked pie shell. Bake for 25 to 30 minutes, or until the custard is set.

Serves 4 humans or one dragon.

Bananas are strictly tropical, but Alzar likes them so much that he cast a little spell so that a banana plant would bear fruit on his mountain. His favorite way to eat bananas is with cream, but he also enjoys baking banana bread and the following pie.

BANANA PIE

1 9-inch pie shell, baked (see page 21), or Graham Cracker Crust (recipe follows)
⅔ cup honey or maple syrup (or ¾ cup turbinado sugar or brown sugar)
¼ cup cornstarch
⅛ teaspoon salt
3 cups milk (with honey use only 2¾ cups milk)
4 eggs, separated
1 tablespoon butter
1 to 1½ teaspoons vanilla
1½ envelopes unflavored gelatin
1 cup heavy cream
3 bananas, sliced
1 banana, sliced
1 pint or more strawberries
Juice of ½ lemon
⅓ cup apple jelly or apricot jam

Mix together the honey, cornstarch, salt, 2½ cups milk, and the egg yolks. In a saucepan cook the mixture over low heat until it forms a thick custard. Take the custard off the burner and add the butter and vanilla. Soften the gelatin in the remaining ½ cup of milk and add it to the custard. Chill the custard until it is cool but not cold. Beat the egg whites until they are stiff, then fold them into the custard. Beat the heavy cream until it is stiff and fold it into the custard along with the banana slices. Spoon the custard into the prepared crust and chill until it is set. Allow at least 2 hours. To decorate, slice the banana into the lemon juice (this keeps bananas from darkening). Arrange the bananas and strawberries attractively to cover the top of the pie. Melt the jelly over the low heat and brush the fruit with the warm jelly to form a glaze.

Serves one dragon plus a piece for Alzar, or 6 to 8 humans.

Graham Cracker Crust
10 graham crackers, crushed fine
4 tablespoons melted butter
2 tablespoons brown sugar or honey
1 teaspoon ground cardamom
¼ teaspoon allspice

Preheat the oven to 400°.
Process all the ingredients together in a processor or blender. Press the crumbs into a 10-inch pie pan. Bake for five to ten minutes. Let the crust cool completely before filling.

A trip to the Coral Lagoon, where the merpeople reside, is always a treat for the wizard and his flying reptile. The dragon loves to play and swim with the merchildren. In one game Neby soars through the air with a rider hanging on for dear life. Then the dragon will allow himself to plunge into the water, taking his delighted passenger with him. All the youngsters clamor for an excursion into the skies. Afterward Neby gobbles up all the fish that the merpeople can prepare for him. Following lunch he settles into a banana-leaf nest made for him by his friends for his afternoon nap. Alzar, on the other hand, stays on shore and views the fun, fishes on the bank, and takes a nap himself. After dinner is served, he presents his hosts with a special dessert he has brought for the occasion.

CITRUS SURPRISE PIE

1 9-inch pie shell, unbaked (page 21)
6 extra large eggs
¼ teaspoon salt
1 cup honey
⅔ cup fresh lemon juice (you may substitute frozen juice, but not bottled)
2 teaspoons grated lemon rind
1½ cups water
Topping (recipe follows) or Most Divine Topping (page 81)

Preheat oven to 425°.

With an electric mixer beat together the eggs, salt, honey, lemon juice, lemon rind, and water for 5 minutes.

Pour the mixture into the unbaked pie shell and bake for 25 minutes. Then reduce the oven to 275° for 5 to 10 minutes, or until the center is set. Test by inserting knife into center; if it comes out clean, the pie is ready.

Cool completely, then refrigerate.

Serves 8 humans, or 4 merpersons, or one dragon, plus a piece for Alzar.

Topping

1½ pints whipping cream
1 tablespoon honey
½ teaspoon vanilla or almond flavoring
1 pint strawberries, cleaned and coarsely chopped
Strawberries, whole or sliced, for decoration (optional)

Beat the cream, honey, and vanilla together until the cream begins to stiffen. Add the strawberries and continue beating until the cream is stiff.

Spread the topping over the cool pie. The pie may be decorated with extra whole or sliced strawberries, or tiny pink or red rose buds, if desired.

For his special friend, Aureena the fairy queen, Alzar makes a wonderful sauce that he serves on fruit. It is impossible to describe and equally impossible to duplicate, because the recipe is a secret. Here is an approximation of this Most Divine Topping, which could be served on anything from fruit to pudding to ice cream.

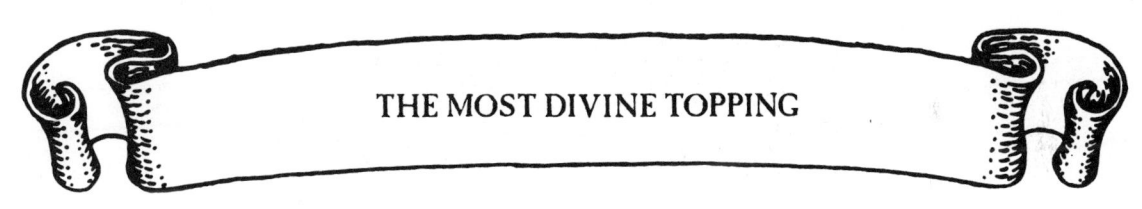

THE MOST DIVINE TOPPING

1½ tablespoons crème de cassis
1 cup heavy cream
1 tablespoon honey
1 cup fresh raspberries, mashed, or frozen raspberries

Combine the crème de cassis, heavy cream, and honey and whip until the mixture is stiff. Fold in the raspberries.
Chill until ready to serve.

Serves 6 humans, or 2 dwarfs, or 2 Amazons, but it's not nearly enough for one dragon.

The light texture of sponge and angel food cakes makes them Alzar's favorite cakes. He may serve them at teatime or after one of his many musical sessions. One of his special recipes is for Lemon-Fennel Cake.

LEMON-FENNEL CAKE

6 eggs, separated
¼ cup fresh lemon juice
¾ teaspoon crushed fennel seeds
1 tablespoon Pernod or anisette (optional)
1 cup turbinado sugar
1 cup less 2 tablespoons unbleached flour or ½ cup whole-wheat and ½ cup unbleached flour
½ teaspoon salt
½ teaspoon cream of tartar

Preheat the oven to 325°.

In an electric mixer beat the egg yolks until they are thick and lemon-colored.

Add the lemon juice, fennel seeds, Pernod, and the ½ cup of sugar. Continue beating at the lowest speed while adding the flour. The batter will be stiff. Set it aside.

In a separate bowl beat the egg whites until they are frothy, then add the salt and cream of tartar. Beat the whites until they are stiff but not dry. One way to test them is to run a spatula through the whites; if they hold their shape they are ready.

Mix ⅓ of the egg whites into the egg yolk–flour batter. Then fold in the remaining whites

Pour the batter into an ungreased 10-inch tube pan and bake for one hour. When done, hang the pan upside down until the cake cools completely before removing it from the pan.

Frost with chocolate icing, or serve with anisette-flavored whipped cream or hot semisweet chocolate sauce.

Serves 8 to 10 humans, many elves, or 2 or possibly 3 Amazons, or 2 dwarfs, or one dragon with a small piece for Alzar.

Famed for his spectacular light show displays and wise counsel, Alzar also enjoys celebrity status for his parties. A gracious host who entertains with many specialty dishes, the wizard never gives dinner parties as such but regales his guests with little teas. The main reason he refrains from giant dinner parties is that he himself eats only the smallest amounts of food, but he does so many times a day.

For his special tea parties he whips up delectable sweets. When the elf princess, Halissa, visits, she requests Princess Cake — named after her. One of its main ingredients, the cheese, is made by the elves. The elves themselves make a type of cheesecake using carob and maple syrup. However, this one is the wizard's version.

PRINCESS CAKE

4 large eggs
1⅓ cups turbinado sugar or 1 cup plus 1 tablespoon honey or 1⅓ cups brown sugar
7 tablespoons cocoa
1 tablespoon vanilla
16 ounces cream cheese
2 pounds sour cream
Crust and Topping (recipes follow)

Preheat oven to 350°.

Beat the eggs and sugar together until they are light in color and thick. Mix in the cocoa and vanilla.

Add the cream cheese in small pieces and beat until smooth. Mix in the sour cream. Then pour the filling into the crust.

Bake for one hour and 30 minutes or until the edge is set and the center is still glossy.

Cool the cake completely before removing it from the springform pan. It is best served the next day.

Spread the cream-cheese topping over the cake.

Serves 10 to 12 humans, or one dragon, or innumerable elves, or 4 Amazons, or 2 dwarfs

Crust

10 graham crackers, crumbled
1 ounce semisweet chocolate, grated
1 teaspoon cinnamon
4 tablespoons melted butter

Mix the graham cracker crumbs, grated chocolate, and cinnamon together. Stir in the melted butter.

Press the mixture onto the bottom and up the sides of a 10-inch springform pan.

To make the crust using a food processor, combine slightly crushed crackers, a piece of chocolate, and cinnamon, and process for about a minute, until all ingredients are thoroughly crushed and mixed. Add the melted butter and process again to mix thoroughly. Press the mixture in a pan as described above.

Topping

3 ounces cream cheese
½ cup whipping cream
⅛ to ¼ cup turbinado sugar, brown sugar, or honey
1½ tablespoons cocoa liqueur

Beat the cream cheese in an electric mixer. Gradually add the cream. Then add the sugar along with the liqueur. Mix thoroughly.

Those who visit Alzar at his mountaintop home must always send a message beforehand, or they might find no one there. Well, not exactly; there is always a feeling that someone is watching, even if no one can be seen. Although it is true that Alzar can make himself invisible, it is also true that he spends as much time away as he does at home. He visits with everyone in Zir — the good and, sometimes, the not so good — and when he calls on his friends, the wizard frequently brings tokens of his affection. Often these presents are as simple as unusual stones or seashells; rarely are they extravagant. However, they always delight their recipients. If Alzar plans to arrive at mealtime, he will bring the dessert. His very favorite treat for gifts or for his own parties is this recipe.

ALZAR'S PARTY TORTE

½ cup butter
¾ cup turbinado sugar or honey or brown sugar
1 teaspoon vanilla
4 large or extra large eggs, separated (medium if honey is used)
3 tablespoons flour or arrowroot (arrowroot makes a lighter cake)
2¼ teaspoons baking powder
¼ teaspoon salt
1 cup warm milk
2¼ cups graham cracker crumbs
Pinch of cream of tartar
Frosting (recipe follows)

Preheat the oven to 350°

Beat the butter, brown sugar, and vanilla until light. Add the egg yolks one at a time.

Mix together the flour or arrowroot, baking powder, and salt. In a separate bowl combine the warm — not hot — milk and the graham cracker crumbs. Alternately add the crumbs and the dry ingredients by thirds to the butter-egg mixture.

Beat the egg whites with the cream of tartar until they are stiff but not dry. Fold one-third of the egg whites into the batter, then fold in the remainder.

Pour the batter into four prepared 8-inch pans or three 9-inch pans. Bake for 20 minutes (8-inch pans) or 25 to 30 minutes (9-inch pans). Cool the layers thoroughly before frosting.

Spread the frosting between the layers and over the top and sides of the cake. Decorate the cake with extra shaved chocolate and/or chopped nuts. Filberts are especially nice.

Chill thoroughly; it's even better when served a day or two after baking.

Serves 8 to 12 humans.

Frosting
    1 cup unsalted butter (raw-milk butter, if possible)
    ½ cup brown or turbinado sugar that has been powdered in a blender, processor, or grinder
    2 egg yolks
    1 teaspoon vanilla or ¾ teaspoon vanilla and ¼ teaspoon almond extract
    4 ounces sweet chocolate, grated
    2 ounces semisweet chocolate, grated
    Chopped nuts (optional)

Beat the butter and sugar together until light. Add the egg yolks, then the vanilla and grated chocolates.

On a visit to Verderoc, Alzar and Neby arrived during a birthday celebration. The reptile was thrilled and very impressed. When the two got back to the mountain, Neby let Alzar know that he would like to have a birthday party. The wizard ignored him, but the dragon persisted. Finally Alzar relented, and he planned a magnificent party for the pesty dragon.

Alzar invited all the children he could fit into his house. The rooms were hung with every decoration a sorcerer can muster. (Many of our customary party hats, streamers, favors, and balloons were first conjured up at the dragon's party.)

After the party the dragon was so tired that he slept for one solid day. The children enjoyed playing games such as hide-and-seek with

THE DWARFS

THE AMAZONS

ALZAR THE WIZARD

THE ELVES

THE TROLLS

THE FAIRIES

THE MERPEOPLE

ZORMENA'S CASTLE

him and riding on his back. To honor Neby further, the wizard gave each child a dragon-shaped kite to take home.

For the party Alzar prepared all of Neby's favorite foods, and for the finale he created a magnificent rolled cake with sauce. Now, the wizard only serves this cake to his special friends. Here it is.

NEBY'S HAPPY BIRTHDAY CAKE

¼ cup unbleached or whole-wheat flour
3½ tablespoons cocoa
¼ teaspoon salt
1 cup of brown or turbinado sugar that has been powdered in a blender, processor, or grinder
5 extra large eggs, separated
½ teaspoon cream of tartar
¾ teaspoon vanilla
Filling and Sauce (recipes follow)

Preheat the oven to 325°.

In a bowl mix the flour, cocoa, salt, and ½ cup of sugar with a wire whisk.

Beat the egg yolks until they are light and lemon-colored. Mix them into the dry ingredients.

Beat the egg whites until they are foamy, then add the cream of tartar. Gradually add the remaining ¼ cup of sugar and finally the vanilla. Thoroughly fold ⅓ of the egg whites into the cocoa batter; then fold in the remainder.

Pour the batter into a jelly-roll pan (approximately 10 × 15 inches) that has been greased and floured, and line it with greased and floured waxed paper.

Bake for 20 to 25 minutes. Cool for 5 to 6 minutes.

Turn the cake onto a clean towel that has been sprinkled with the 4 tablespoons of powdered brown sugar. Pull off the waxed paper. Trim the sides of the cake and roll it up lengthwise in the towel. Allow the cake to cool completely, then unroll it.

Spread the filling over the unrolled cake and reroll it. Place the cake on a serving platter.

Top each portion of the cake with this bittersweet sauce. The sauce should be very hot when served.

Serves one dragon, or 6 to 8 humans, depending on the size of the serving.

Filling
- 1 cup whipping cream
- 2 tablespoons honey
- 1 teaspoon vanilla

Whip the cream, honey, and vanilla together with an electric mixer until the cream is stiff.

Sauce
- 8 ounces semisweet chocolate
- 1 ounce unsweetened chocolate
- ½ to ¾ cup cream

Melt the chocolate with the cream in a double boiler and heat until the sauce is hot. Do not boil. The thickness of the sauce can be controlled by adding more cream or chocolate.

In the years and centuries that follow, Alzar will grow in wisdom and power. No one knows what future he sees for Zir, but it is certain that Neby will be there at his side testing the wizard's patience every step of the way.

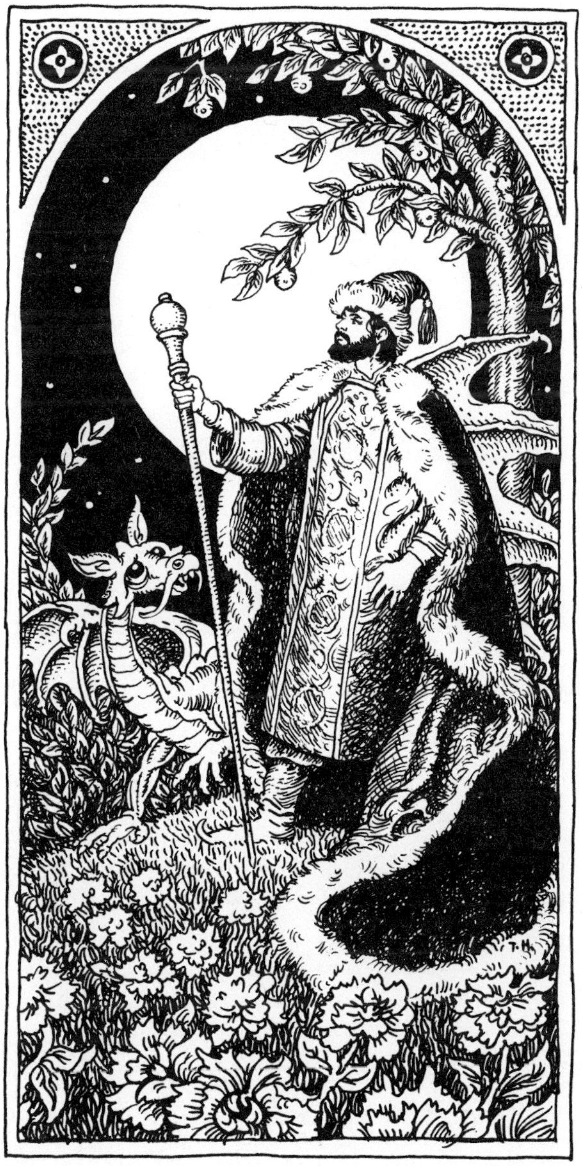

THE ELVES

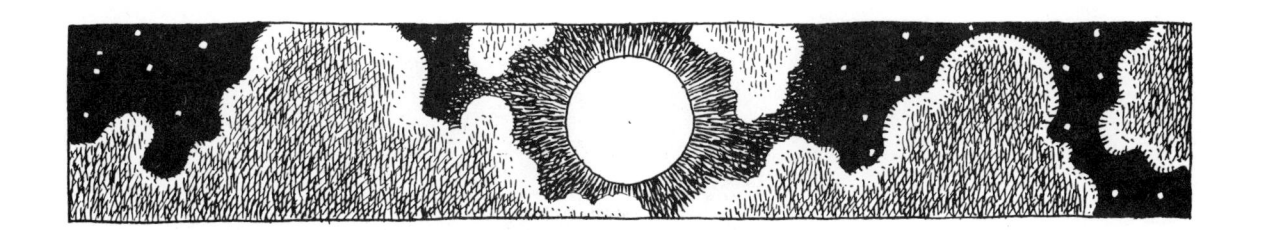

As the light of the full moon glistens on the silvery archway over the entrance to Elvinor, the city of the elves, it reveals the secret of their way of life. The inscription on the gate reads "⟨inscription⟩", which in the common language of Zir means "The road to adventure through service to all of life."

Drifting out from the Forest of Freen are the mystical sounds of the partying elves. They greet the night with a burst of song and music. The light from the moon casts a cool glow over the silver mushroom city and reveals the elves dancing, eating, and making merry. At dawn the city will disappear from sight, but the elves will continue with their activities. Each day they work as hard as they played the night before. When day comes there are new places to visit, as they treat the sick and injured creatures or care for the many plants and trees of Zir. This labor is the elfin adventure.

Life also continues joyously in the elves' invisible city as their market opens each dawn. The produce is laid out like the exuberant colors of a patchwork quilt. All types of foods, vegetables, fruits, breads, grains, cheeses, and eggs are displayed and sold or traded — everything, that is, but meats, for the elves are vegetarians.

Elves only sleep for two or three hours a day, which they do in the afternoon. Following their rest, the day of work and play continues.

Along with the white elves who live in the mushroom city, the Forest of Freen is haven to the felves. These cousins to the white elves are a type of miniature wood elf. They live in hollowed-out tree stumps or under the roots of the great trees in the forest. They are secretive people and only a few things are known about their life-style. They live in small family groups, marry late in life, and usually have only one or two children. Felves mainly care for the small creatures of the fields and forest and sustain themselves by gathering grains, seeds, greens, and fruits. Their eating habits are very much like those of their white, city-dwelling elf cousins.

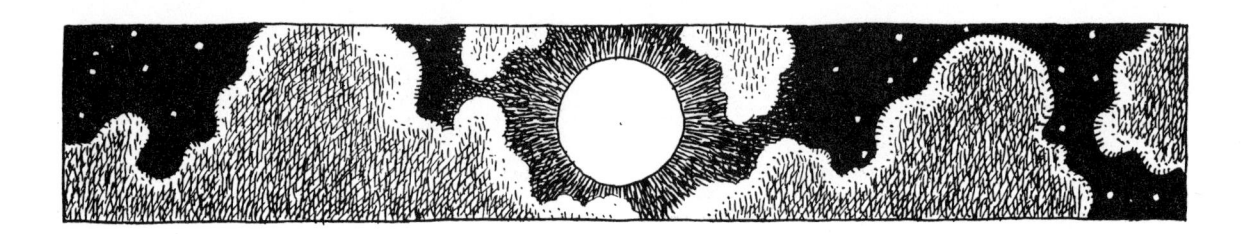

In contrast to the felves, the city elves live in large family groups, each sharing a mushroom house, which grows to accommodate any increase in numbers. Their society is ruled by a prince and princess who are appointed to their office for life, but the couple usually resigns after a time in order to give others the honor of ruling. Some couples are reappointed. Prince Timmeken and Princess Tira have served many times.

This couple's power is absolute, but always just. They act as hosts to visitors and coordinate all the activities of elfin life. The rulers live in a separate, though not opulent, house and wear clothes similar to those of all the other elves. Except for the golden circlet on their heads, one could not tell them from any other elf. For the elves the role of ruler is a position of honor and responsibility, not of wealth.

Both communities of elves are vegetarians and basically eat fruits, vegetables, nuts, grains and legumes; however, they also include dairy products and eggs in their diet.

The elves eat two main meals a day, one in the late morning and the other at their nightly feast. They do not, however, confine their eating to those times. As a matter of fact, they love to snack on sweets, fruit drinks, tea, or their marvelous cheeses.

A morning meal may include bread, fruit — fresh or stewed — some kind of soufflé or cheese, certainly a salad, perhaps even a vegetable, and dessert accompanied by an herb tea. Portions are not large, but a variety of food is always available, because the elves' communal cooking arrangement offers an opportunity for each cook to prepare a specialty item.

The evening meal contains even more variety, because many households join together to produce a feast. Elves always serve rolls or muffins as well as salads and an array of cooked vegetables prepared plain or in sauces. Grains alone or in combinations with legumes are a must, as are cheeses and eggs. Elves raise birds that lay colorful eggs. (Humans must have borrowed the idea of coloring eggs from them.) Then come the desserts. All during this extended meal the elves drink tea. If there are visitors, tea is served, as well as a fruit or milk drink.

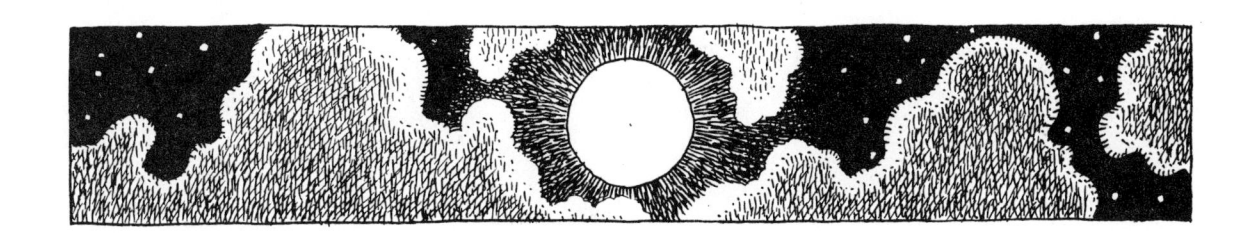

Although the foods they cook are very delicious, the elves do not use recipes, except when it comes to dessert. They cook simply by steaming, baking, or sautéing their food. They are more interested in what goes on at their communal feast than in the food they have prepared. It is the music, dancing, recitations, conversations, even exhibitions of crafts and hobbies, that command their attention.

Still, no woodland banquet would be complete without some type of dip and crackers. Here's a combination that is perfect for human parties, too.

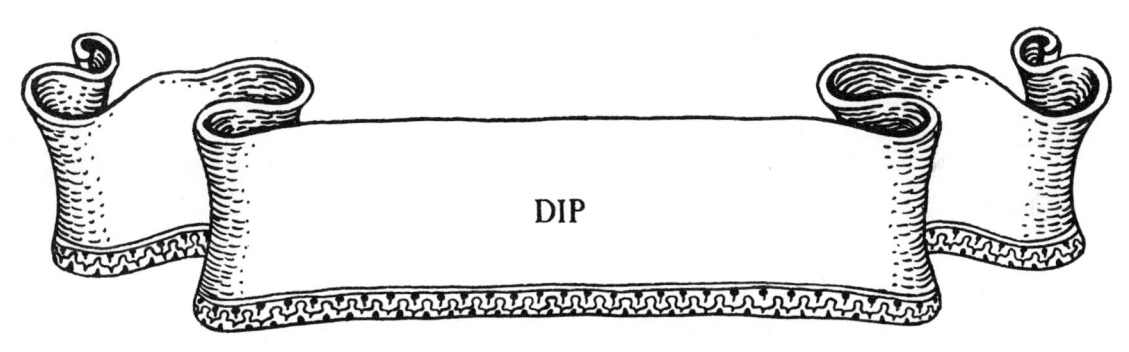

DIP

16 ounces sour cream
1 tablespoon plus 1 teaspoon freeze dried chives or 1½ teaspoons fresh chives
¼ teaspoon coriander leaves
¼ teaspoon ground coriander seeds
½ teaspoon onion powder
1½ teaspoons finely minced crystallized ginger
2 teaspoons minced fresh ginger
¼ teaspoon garlic salt

Mix all the ingredients together in a small bowl. Allow the dip to sit in the refrigerator for at least half an hour before serving so that the flavors will blend.

Serve with whole-wheat crackers, rice cakes, or oat crackers (*recipe follows*). Leftover dip, if there is any, is delicious on hot noodles or baked potatoes.

Serves many elves and 8 to 12 humans.

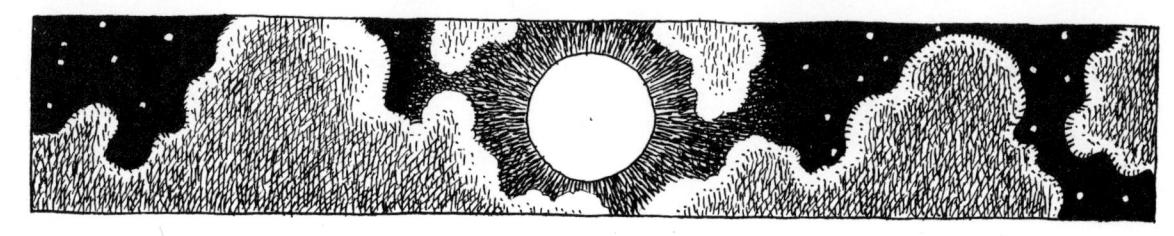

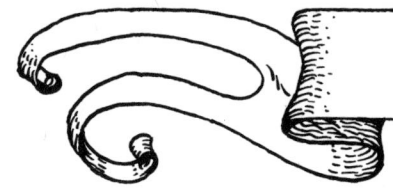

OAT CRACKERS

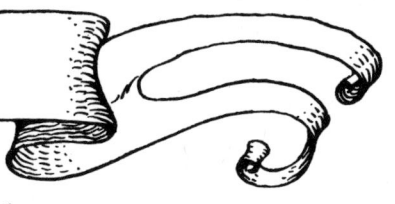

2 cups ground oatmeal
½ cup unbleached flour
¼ cup oil
1 teaspoon salt
½ cup water, milk, or yogurt
2 teaspoons tamari

Preheat oven to 375°.

Mix the dry ingredients with the wet ingredients by hand or with a food processor. Roll out the dough until it is very thin and cut it into round or square cracker shapes.

Bake the cracker dough on a cookie sheet for 8 minutes. Turn off the oven and leave the crackers in for half an hour to crisp.

Cool and store the crackers in a covered container.

Makes about 3½ dozen crackers, depending on size.

Throughout the year the forest and woods are kept clear of fallen trees. The elves work cutting, hauling, and stacking the logs. Often they carry this wood to other parts of Zir for use by those who do not live near a forest. Helping the elf workers are black, doglike animals called Peeks, who are hitched to log-laden wagons or sleds. (More about Peeks later.) Much of this work takes place in winter, and to warm themselves and their beasts the elves will boil up some Trail Soup and serve it with bread brought from the city. Many different herbs and vegetables can be used to make this soup. The elves carry some of the ingredients with them, but they also use whatever fresh foods are available in the area.

TRAIL SOUP

1 cup onions, sliced
1 tablespoon oil or butter
1 cup carrots sliced in rounds
1 cup celery
½ cup green or red bell peppers, cut in strips
1½ cups cabbage, sliced
½ teaspoon pepper
½ teaspoon basil
½ teaspoon thyme
5 cups water
4 tablespoons miso

Miso can be purchased at oriental food stores or health food shops. You can use 5 cups of chicken stock in place of miso and water, but then it is no longer a vegetarian soup.

Sauté the onions in oil or butter until they are limp.

Add the carrots, celery, and bell peppers, and sauté one minute longer. Then add the cabbage, pepper, basil, thyme, and water.

Simmer until vegetables are tender but still crisp.

Add the miso and heat the soup through, but do not boil.

Serve at once with noodles; homemade are preferable, but Japanese buckwheat noodles are also nice. This soup is also good with whole-wheat crackers or bread.

Serves 6 to 8.

The crowning of a new elf prince and princess means a special ceremonial party with a visit from Alzar the wizard and his dragon, Neby, and Aureena, the fairy queen, and her court. The elves always prepare gifts for their visitors, usually jewelry fashioned from the silver mushrooms and exotic stones made with elfin magic. Neby is particularly fond of the sparkling jewels, so he gets a great big one, which he plays with like a ball.

The coronation festivities take place at the summer solstice, and the main entrée is Broccoli Puff, a very special soufflé.

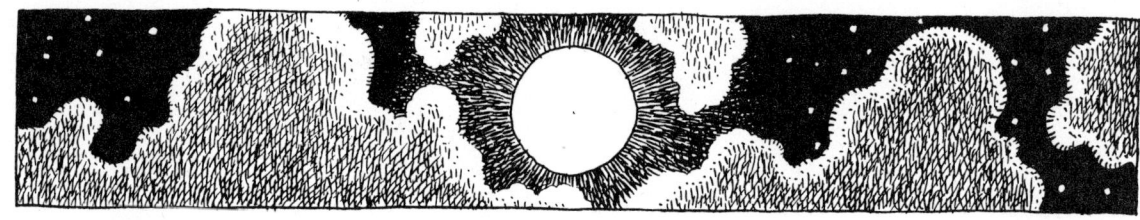

BROCCOLI PUFF

5 to 6 new red potatoes (enough for 1½ cups puree)
5 tablespoons flour
4 tablespoons butter
1¼ teaspoon salt
¼ teaspoon pepper
2 cups hot milk
6 extra large eggs or 7 large eggs, separated
1 cup broccoli flowerets, minced
¾ cup cheddar cheese, shredded

Preheat oven to 375°.

Double lengthwise a piece of aluminum foil long enough to completely circumscribe a 6-cup soufflé. Butter one side. With kitchen string, tie foil onto the soufflé pan, buttered side in, to form a collar extending 3½ inches higher than the pan rim.

Boil the potatoes until they are tender. Puree them in a blender or food processor.

Make a roux with the flour, butter, salt, and pepper. Cook it gently for 2 to 3 minutes. Add the hot milk, stirring constantly with a whisk, and cook until thick.

Add a little of the white sauce to the egg yolks to heat them. Pour the egg-yolk mixture into the white sauce and cook one minute longer. Remove the sauce from the burner.

Stir in the pureed potatoes, broccoli, and cheddar cheese.

Beat the egg whites, then fold them into the sauce. Pour the mixture into the prepared soufflé dish.

Bake for one hour and 10 minutes. When soufflé is done, remove collar and serve immediately.

Serves 4 to 6 humans, or 10 to 12 elves.

The elves invented the next recipe to honor the wizard's first visit to Elvinor. It is truly a light and wonderful waffle. Once you taste it, you will never be satisfied with any other waffle.

WIZARD WAFFLES

1 cup rice flour
1 cup potato starch or flour (arrowroot or tapioca starch may also be used)
1½ teaspoons baking soda
1 tablespoon vegetable oil

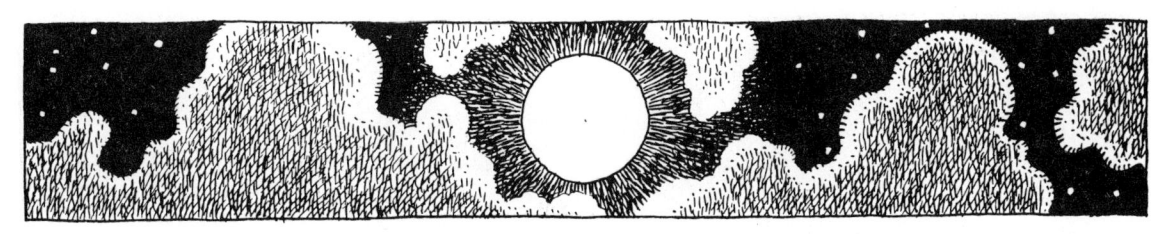

½ teaspoon baking powder
½ teaspoon salt
2 eggs, beaten
2-pound (32 ounces) container of plain yogurt
Maple Butter (recipes follow)

Preheat the waffle iron. With a wire whisk blend together the dry ingredients. In a bowl, beat the eggs, then add the yogurt. Beat in the dry ingredients and oil. The batter is now ready for the waffle iron. This batter can also be made into pancakes. Serve with Maple Butter, jam, or use the waffles as a base for creamed foods or ice-cream desserts.

Serves 4 to 6 humans, or 10 to 15 wood elves.

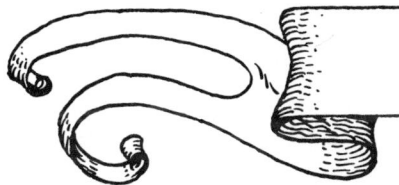

MAPLE BUTTER

¼ pound hard butter
½ cup whipping cream
1½ cups maple syrup

Place the butter in the bowl of an electric mixer and beat at low speed until it is soft. Add the whipping cream. Beat for 3 to 5 minutes.

Add the maple syrup, ½ cup at a time, and beat for about 5 minutes.

To serve, press the butter mixture through a pastry tube onto butter plates. It is delicious with hot rolls, waffles, or toast.

MAPLE BUTTER II

¼ pound butter
1 cup maple syrup

In a blender or food processor or with an electric mixer, beat together the butter and maple syrup until creamy. Stores indefintely in refrigerator.

The silver mushrooms provide (with a little assistance from the elves) the cloth from which the white city elves make their clothing. Not only does the wondrous cloth keep the elves warm in winter and cool in the summer, but their apparel also changes colors with each season, so that the elves blend into their surroundings. And as if that were not enough, their garments become a blaze of rainbow colors and sparkle with jewellike brilliance when the elves are in the mood for celebration and begin to sing and dance.

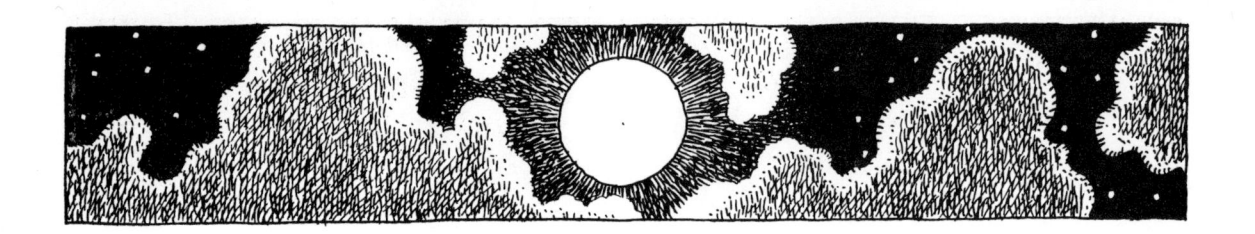

In honor of the magic silver mushrooms the elves created this dish made from ordinary mushrooms.

MOONLIGHT MUSHROOMS

1½ pounds large mushrooms, with stems removed
⅓ cup oil or melted butter
3½ tablespoons butter, melted
¼ to ⅓ cup minced onions
¾ teaspoon curry powder
1½ tablespoons flour
¾ cup hot milk or half-and-half
2 eggs, separated
½ teaspoon salt, or to taste
½ teaspoon pepper, or to taste
½ to ¾ cup cooked and mashed vegetables, such as eggplant (fresh whole-wheat bread crumbs can be substituted, if desired)

Preheat the oven to 400°.

Clean the mushrooms; remove the stems and save them for other use. Brush the mushroom caps with oil or butter and place them top down in a baking pan.

In a skillet sauté the onions in melted butter for two minutes. Add the curry powder and flour and cook for 3 minutes. Add the hot milk or half-and-half.

When the mixture has thickened, remove the pan from the heat. Beat the egg yolks, then add some of the sauce to the yolks. Pour the yolks into the sauce and return the pan to the heat. Cook for 1 minute.

Add the salt, pepper, and the cooked vegetables or crumbs. Remove the mixture from the heat.

In a bowl beat the egg whites until they are stiff but not dry. Fold the egg whites into the vegetable mixture.

Fill mushroom tops with the mixture. Bake for 12 to 15 minutes.

Serves 15 to 20 as an hors d'oeuvre or first course for humans

Within the city walls there is a variety of magical industries to keep the elves busy. They work with all types of materials, even jewels, and are particularly proud of their special bows and arrows, which are fashioned from the dead hulls of the silver mushrooms. These bows and arrows are used as protection against the goblins, trolls, and other unpleasant creatures that lurk in the mountains and caverns of Zir. When one of these creatures is struck by an arrow, he instantly becomes nicer. If he is hit three times, the unpleasant creature becomes hopelessly good and can never return to his old ways. The elves then take the reformed goblin or troll and teach him to care for himself and help with the elfin work.

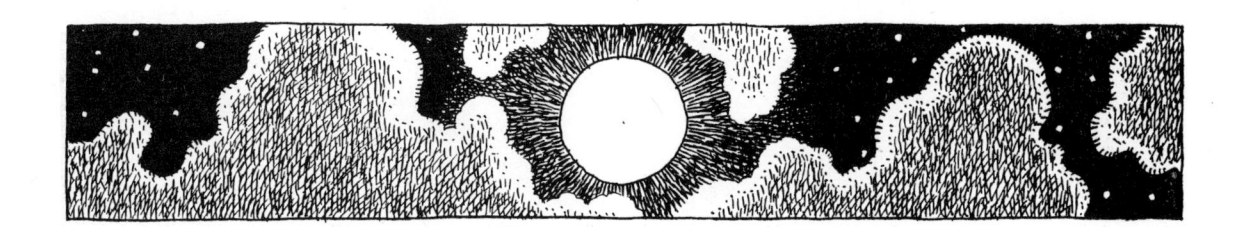

One of the recipes the elves teach to their new friends is Vegetables in the Oven, which is a simple casserole.

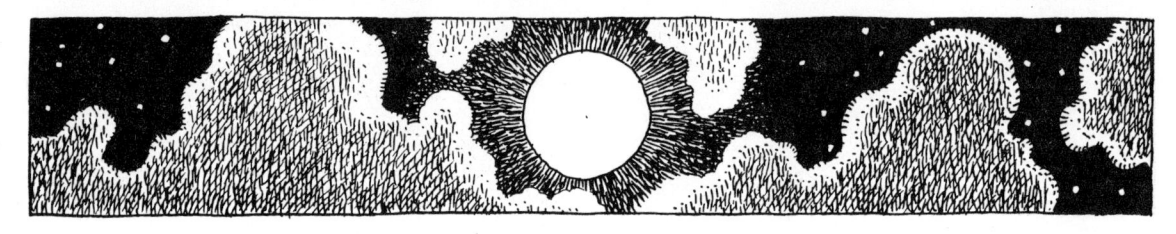

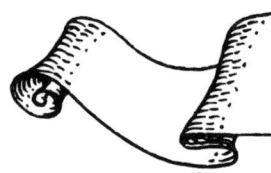

VEGETABLES IN THE OVEN

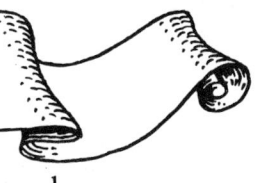

3 cups cooked broccoli, chopped into 1-inch pieces (celery, green green beans, or lima beans can be substituted)
¼ to ½ cup slivered almonds
½ cup water chestnuts
7 tablespoons butter
3 tablespoons flour
1 cup vegetable or chicken broth (or ½ cup vegetable and ½ cup chicken broth)
¾ cup half-and-half
½ to ¾ cup mushrooms, sliced
½ cup freshly grated Parmesan or Romano cheese
½ cup crumbs (shredded wheat, bread crumbs, or corn flakes)
Salt and pepper to taste

Preheat oven to 350°.

In a skillet make a roux using 4 tablespoons of the butter and the flour. When it has cooked and bubbled for one minute, add the broth and the half-and-half. Cook, stirring constantly, over medium heat until thick. Correct the seasoning with salt and pepper and set aside.

In another skillet, sauté the almonds in the remaining butter until they are light golden brown, then remove them from pan. Add the mushrooms to the pan and sauté gently.

In a 2 quart ovenproof casserole dish, layer the broccoli, almonds, water chestnuts, and mushrooms. Pour the cream mixture over the vegetables. Top the casserole with the crumbs and cheese.

Bake for 30 minutes.

Serves 4 to 6 humans or 8 to 10 elves.

The elves often have picnics out in the open on the ground, when they are in a part of Zir that has no large trees. To protect themselves from any harm, the elves first mark the ground with a circle. Every item used at the meal is circular in shape; so are the campfire cloths they spread on the earth. The elves eat in a circle and the foods they serve maintain the same motif. In this way they create a protective ring of power that no creature can penetrate. Foods they eat on these picnics include mushroom caps, muffins, vegetables cut in rounds, or grain cakes.

PICNIC CARROTS

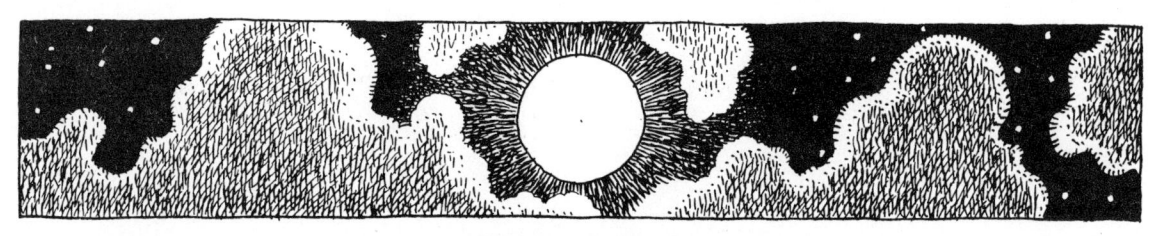

1 pound carrots
Pinch of salt
2 tablespoons butter
2 tablespoons sherry
4 to 8 grates of fresh nutmeg or a pinch of ground nutmeg
4 teaspoons ground mace

Scrub the carrots very well and slice them diagonally about ½-inch thick. Cook until they are just tender in a small amount of salted water. Drain them thoroughly. In a skillet sauté the carrots in butter with nutmeg and mace. Add sherry and let it boil for 2 minutes, spooning the sauce over carrots as they cook. Serve at once.

Serves 4 human, 6 city elves, or 12 felves.

To continue the round motif the elves serve grain patties. Try this one.

GRAIN PATTIES

1 cup millet, rice, or couscous
1 tablespoon oil or butter
1½ teaspoon vegetable salt
⅛ to ¼ teaspoon curry (up to 1½ teaspoons can be added, if desired)
2½ cups boiling water or vegetable stock
½ cup grated carrots
½ cup minced scallions
½ cup minced parsley
¼ cup minced celery or green peppers (optional)
⅓ cup whole-wheat flour
2 tablespoons soy flour
1 tablespoon wheat germ

If millet or rice is used, sauté it in oil until lightly brown. Add the salt, curry powder, boiling water or stock, and the vegetables. If cous-cous is used, boil it in water or stock and add other ingredients. Bring the mixture to a boil, lower the heat, and cover. Simmer for 45 minutes at low heat, until liquid absorbed. Do not stir grain. Remove from the heat and cool. The mixture can be refrigerated overnight.

When ready to prepare the patties for serving, form the mixture into round patties. Dip each patty in a mixture of whole-wheat flour, soy flour, and wheat germ. In a skillet sauté the patties in oil until brown. Keep them hot.

Make a sauce, if desired, by adding a little vegetable stock to the pan. Bring it to a boil and add a dash of soy sauce for flavor.

Serves 4 to 6 humans or 8 to 12 elves, depending on the size of the patties.

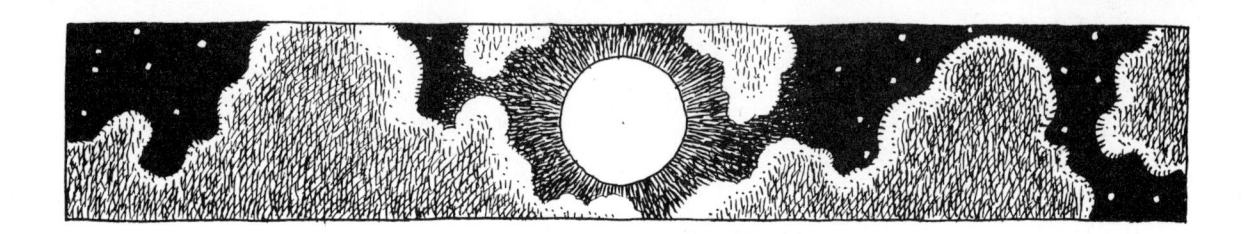

Elves accompany their salads with a variety of herbal dressings. Using every conceivable herb, spice, oil, vinegar, fruit juice, or dairy product to vary their dressing, the elves serve these concoctions not only on salads, but also over cooked vegetables or even noodles and cooked grains.

Fairies use a dressing very much like this recipe, but they vary the herbs and omit the honey.

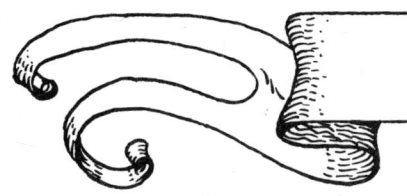

HERBAL DRIZZLE

1 cup oil
½ cup vinegar
2 teaspoons honey
1 teaspoon garlic powder
1½ teaspoon dried minced onions
1 teaspoon salt
¼ teaspoon pepper
1 teaspoon dry mustard
½ teaspoon marjoram
½ teaspoon dried parsley flakes

Place all the ingredients in a blender and mix until thoroughly blended. The recipe can be doubled and kept in the refrigerator indefinitely. Just stir it up before using it.

Makes about 1½ cups.

NOTE: You can omit the honey and include the following herbs, as the fairies do: ¼ teaspoon oregano, ¼ teaspoon thyme, ¼ teaspoon paprika.

The black, doglike animals called Peeks that assist the elves in their ecological efforts work willingly with them. They are repaying an ancestral debt to the elfin society. Their species was on the verge of extinction because the old witch Zormena, whose castle stands in the middle of a terrible swamp, liked to use their fur to cover its floors and walls. One day in his youth, Timmekin, the elves' current prince, ventured into the hag's courtyard and released all the captured Peeks. Then he and a band of elfin youths rode the animals out of the swamp to safety. Since then the Peeks have lived outside Elvinor and work along with the elves.

The elves communicate with the Peeks through telepathy, as they do with all the other animals of Zir. The black animals roam freely in the city, so that the elfin children experience unusual playmates and also enjoy special protectors.

Peeks are basically vegetarians like the elves and usually eat whatever the elf cooks prepare. Elves and dogs alike have a fondness for all types of pickles. One kind, their particular favorite, is made in great abundance from a root much like the Jerusalem artichoke and is named in honor of the black animals — Peek Pickles. These are very simple to prepare.

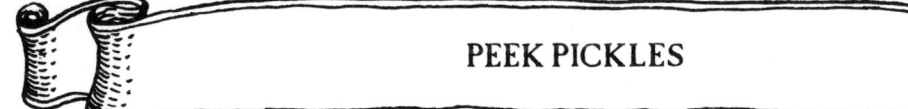

PEEK PICKLES

2 pounds Jerusalem artichokes, cut into 1-inch pieces
1 quart vinegar
⅛ cup salt
1 cup sugar
⅛ cup mustard seeds
1 tablespoon celery seed
½ tablespoon tumeric
1½ teaspoons coriander
1 teaspoon dry mustard
3 slices of ginger root
½-inch piece of dried chili pepper

Scrub the artichokes with a stiff brush and cut them into one-inch pieces. Pack them into sterilized canning jars.

In an enamel pan bring to boil the vinegar, salt, sugar, and spices. Let the mixture cool, then pour it over the artichokes in the jars.

Seal the jars with lids and let them stand one month before using the pickles.

Makes 4 one-pint jars.

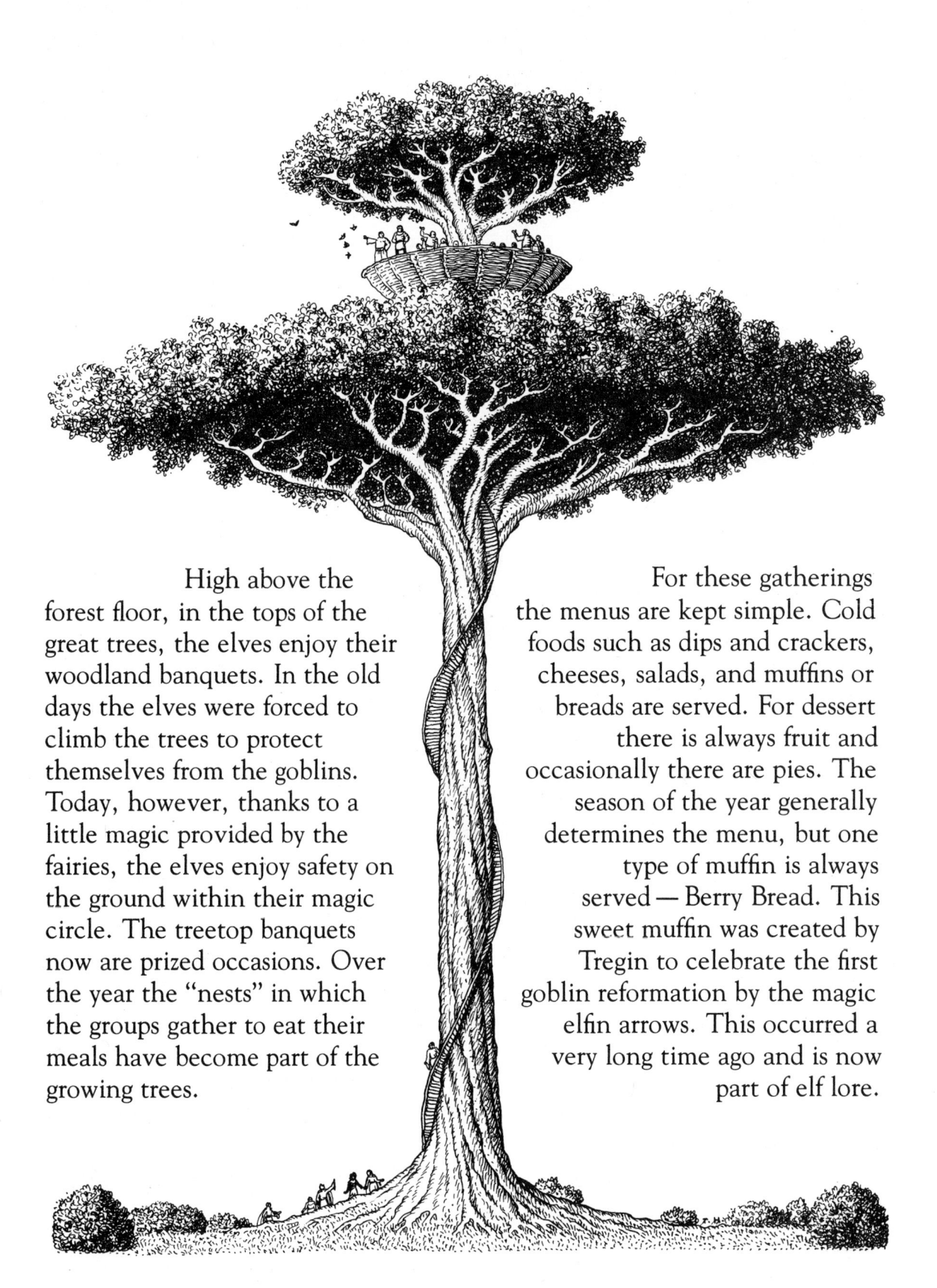

High above the forest floor, in the tops of the great trees, the elves enjoy their woodland banquets. In the old days the elves were forced to climb the trees to protect themselves from the goblins. Today, however, thanks to a little magic provided by the fairies, the elves enjoy safety on the ground within their magic circle. The treetop banquets now are prized occasions. Over the year the "nests" in which the groups gather to eat their meals have become part of the growing trees.

For these gatherings the menus are kept simple. Cold foods such as dips and crackers, cheeses, salads, and muffins or breads are served. For dessert there is always fruit and occasionally there are pies. The season of the year generally determines the menu, but one type of muffin is always served — Berry Bread. This sweet muffin was created by Tregin to celebrate the first goblin reformation by the magic elfin arrows. This occurred a very long time ago and is now part of elf lore.

BERRY BREAD

½ cup sugar or ⅓ cup honey
½ cup butter
2 eggs, beaten
1 cup unbleached white flour
1 cup whole-wheat flour
1 teaspoon cinnamon
1 teaspoon nutmeg
1 teaspoon baking soda
½ cup yogurt or buttermilk
1 cup cranberry sauce (or strawberry jam, apple jelly, or any berry jam)

Preheat the oven to 350°.

Cream together the sugar or honey with the butter until it is creamy. Add the eggs and continue beating until the mixture is light.

In a separate bowl mix together the dry ingredients.

In another bowl fold together the yogurt and cranberry sauce. Alternately fold ¼ of the butter-egg mixture and ¼ of the yogurt mixture into the dry ingredients until all ingredients are combined. Do not overmix.

Spoon the batter into a muffin tin and bake in the oven for 20 minutes.

Makes one dozen human-size muffins or ½ dozen elf-size muffins.

To all the creatures of Zir, good or bad, the elves offer aid. The evil critters usually avoid the elves' help because, unfortunately for them, invariably they not only regain their health under the elves' care, they also gradually become good. Then they cannot return to their own kind. But the elves always provide for such circumstances.

When a creature is found injured or sick the elves will stay and nurse it until it is completely recovered. To those who are unaware, the healing vibrations of the elves' music sounds no different from nature's own noises — a babbling brook, a spring breeze rustling the leaves, or a songbird — but to a sick beast the elf flute or harp resonates the healing notes that soothe the ailing patient.

This work is very draining for the elves, and they usually fast while working their magic. After the patient's recovery, the elves dine heartily on their special cheese puffs.

SPECIAL CHEESE PUFFS

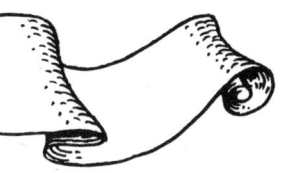

1 pound ricotta cheese
1 pound feta cheese
1 bunch scallions, minced
1 bunch fresh dill, minced
1 package (10 ounces) frozen, chopped spinach, thawed
2 eggs
2 packages frozen puff pastry or phyllo leaves
(1 pound melted butter, if using phyllo leaves)

Drain the feta cheese and crumble it into a bowl. Add the ricotta cheese and all remaining ingredients except the pastry and the butter. Mix thoroughly.

If using puff pastry, roll out the pastry and cut it into squares. Place one teaspoon of cheese mixture in each square and fold it into a triangle. Bake the pastry as directed on the package, or for 5 to 10 minutes at 400°.

If using phyllo leaves, construct the triangular-shaped puffs as follows. Using ½ of the dough at a time, cut it in half lengthwise. Return the remaining amount to the package to keep it from drying out. Spread the top phyllo leaf with melted butter and fold that leaf into thirds lengthwise. This will form a strip of dough that is 3 layers thick. Now, add a teaspoon of cheese mixture at one end of the strip and begin by folding the corner into the shape of a right triangle. Continue folding into triangles from the right side to the left side of the strip, as if folding up a flag, until this strip is finished. The end result is a multilayered triangle. Proceed with the next leaf in the same way. When all the triangles are made, brush the tops with more butter. Bake on a cookie sheet at 375° until they are light brown in color. They will puff slightly. Serve hot.

Serves 15 to 20 as an appetizer.

VARIATION: Cheese-puff mixture can also be used to stuff large mushroom caps. Brush one pound mushroom caps with oil and fill with the cheese mixture. Bake on cookie sheet for 5 to 10 minutes at 350°.

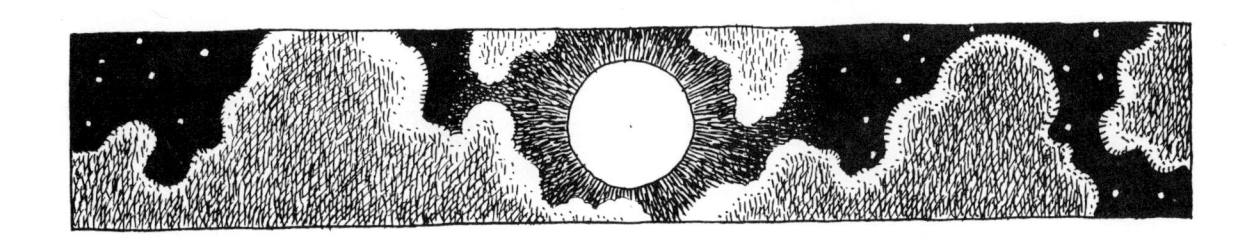

When they are single, both male and female elves cook. However, after their joining or uniting ceremony, the female elf assumes most of the food-preparation duties. Nevertheless, baking bread and rolls remains the domain of the males. The following is a staple in any elf household.

BULGUR ROLLS

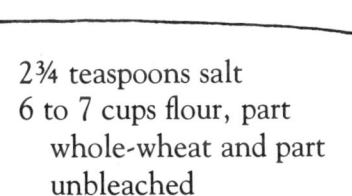

½ cup cracked wheat (bulgur)
1 cup cold water
1 package dry yeast
¼ cup warm water
1¾ cups milk
½ cup plus ½ teaspoon brown sugar or turbinado sugar
2¾ teaspoons salt
6 to 7 cups flour, part whole-wheat and part unbleached
1 egg, slightly beaten
¼ cup salad oil

Soak the cracked wheat in the cold water for several hours or overnight.

When ready to prepare the rolls, dissolve in the warm water, to which ½ teaspoon sugar has been added. Cover and set aside in a warm place to proof.

In a saucepan scald the milk, then cool it to lukewarm. Add the brown sugar and salt and two cups of the flour. (The larger the proportion of unbleached flour to whole-wheat, the lighter will be the texture as well as the color of the rolls.) Beat vigorously until the gluten is formed. (You will know because the batter gets stringy.)

Add the salad oil, salt, egg, and soaked cracked wheat. Continue beating, adding more flour and the proofed yeast until the dough can no longer be beaten.

Turn the dough onto a floured surface and knead in the remaining flour. Knead until the dough is no longer sticky.

Place it in a greased bowl and cover it with a damp towel and plastic wrap. Put it in warm place to rise, about one to 1½ hours, depending on the kitchen atmosphere.

When the dough doubles in bulk, punch it down. Roll it out and cut it into the desired size and shape. Elves usually roll the dough pieces in melted butter, then place them in a greased pan. This makes a richer roll, but it is not necessary. Allow the rolls to rise again until almost double in bulk.

Bake in a preheated oven at 375° for 15 minutes.

Makes 24 small dinner rolls or 12 to 16 wonderful hamburger rolls.

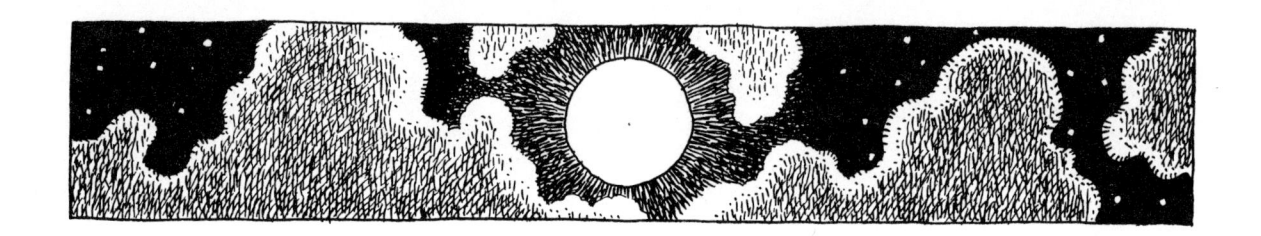

Work trips are always scheduled on a rotation basis so that not all the adult members of a family are away at the same time. After an absence of a week to two months, depending on weather and distance traveled, the returning workers are welcomed home with a party. Naturally, the workers bring back gifts of rare fruits, vegetables, flowers, plants, and beautiful pieces of wood or shells.

With the fruits the elfin women cook a variety of pastries, but the special treat and an elf favorite is Reena's Fruit Yummy. This dish can be a sweet salad or a dessert and is usually served in a crystal bowl. The elves decorate the top with an elaborate floral design made of sliced fruit. The types of fruit used in this recipe vary widely according to the season and availability, but apples, oranges, and nuts are always a part of the concoction.

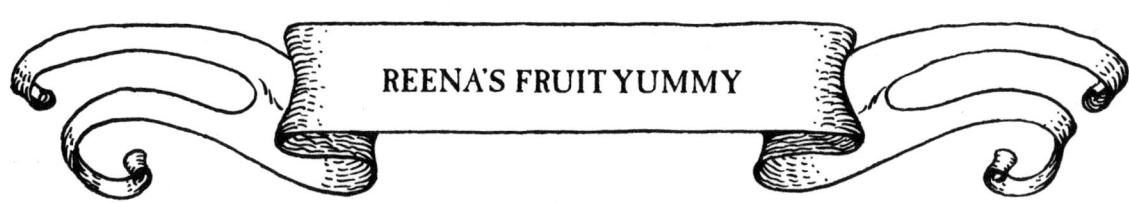

REENA'S FRUIT YUMMY

2 apples, chopped
1 sliced orange, or 8 ounces canned mandarin oranges, drained
1 or 2 bananas, sliced
1 cup canned, crushed pineapple, drained
1 16-ounce can fruit cocktail drained
½ cup dried or grated fresh coconut
¼ cup sliced grapes
½ to 1 cup pecans, chopped
Strawberries, peaches, nectarines or apricots (optional)
1 cup heavy cream
Sauce (recipe follows)

In a large bowl mix the fruit with the nuts and coconut.

Whip the cream until it is stiff. Fold it into the cold custard.

Add the fruits and nuts. Mix thoroughly and chill. Decorate the top with sliced fruits. Serve the same day. This dish may be kept overnight, but it does become watery.

Serves about 8 to 10 humans or 30 elves.

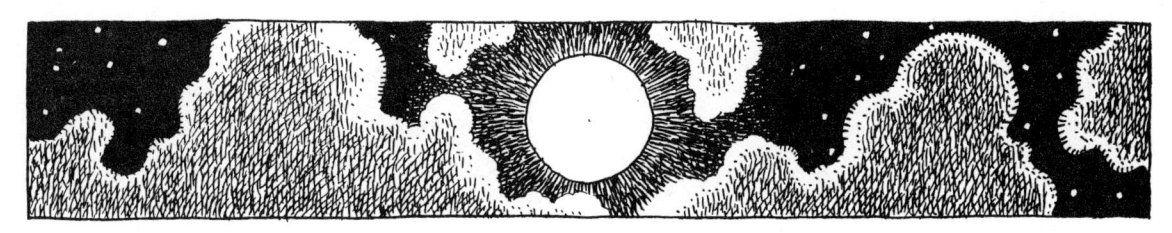

Sauce

2 cups milk	4 tablespoons flour
¾ to 1 cup honey or brown sugar	1 egg, beaten
	1 teaspoon vanilla

Mix the milk, honey, and flour together in a saucepan and cook over medium heat until the mixture boils and thickens. Remove the pan from the burner and add ½ cup of the custard mixture to the beaten egg. Then return the egg mixture to the custard sauce.

Return the pan to the stove and cook over medium heat for 1 minute. Allow the custard to cool, then add vanilla. Refrigerate until cold.

Elves love puddings and tarts. They even prefer them to cakes. Throughout its long history, this recipe was traditionally served as a pudding for snacks or at breakfast, but it tastes equally delicious as a pie.

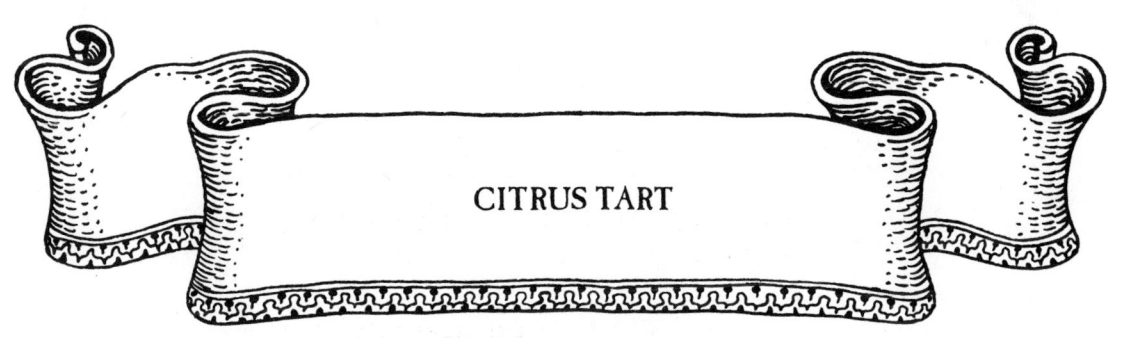

CITRUS TART

⅔ to ¾ cup honey	3 egg whites
2 tablespoons butter, melted	1 9-inch pie shell, unbaked (page 21)
Grated rind and juice of 2 lemons	Whipped cream, grated lemon rind, or grated nutmeg (optional)
3 egg yolks	
3 tablespoons flour	
1 cup milk or water	

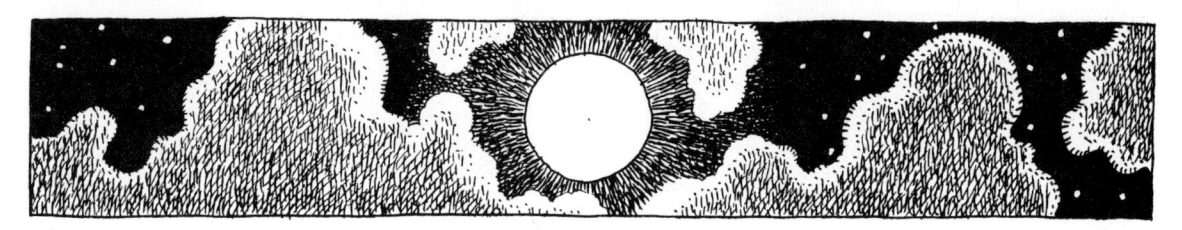

Preheat oven to 425°.

In a bowl, beat together honey, butter, lemon rind, lemon juice, and egg yolks. In a separate bowl, mix together the flour and milk, adding the milk very gradually to the flour so that no lumps will form. Add the flour mixture to the honey-lemon mixture. Set aside.

Beat the egg whites until they are stiff but not dry. Fold the beaten egg whites into the lemon-milk mixture and pour it into the unbaked pie shell. Bake at 425° for 10 minutes, then lower the temperature to 350° for 20 to 30 minutes, until the filling is set. The pie is done when a knife inserted into its center comes out clean.

The pie will have a spongelike top layer with lemon custard underneath. Serve very cold. It may be iced with a thin layer of whipped cream and sprinkled with grated lemon rind or grated nutmeg.

This recipe may also be made into individual tarts. Place the filling in uncooked pastry tart shells and reduce the baking time accordingly.

Other citrus juices may be used instead of lemon. With lime juice use 4 eggs, the juice of 2 limes, and one to 1¼ cups honey.

Serves 6 to 8 humans or 10 to 12 elves.

Along with their care of plants the elves have also developed many new species of fruits, flowers, and even trees through grafting, pollinization, and some magic. Their varieties of apples are endless. They have even developed a type called Tamgo, which grows in the tropical region.

A favorite elfin fruit, apples are eaten every way possible. The elves' imaginative apple recipes are featured during the Autumn Festival of Colors. After the elfin children make their traditional treasure hunt to collect the russet, gold, and orange leaves that have fallen from the trees, all of the elves settle down to admire their finds and to enjoy a helping or two of Autumn Tarts.

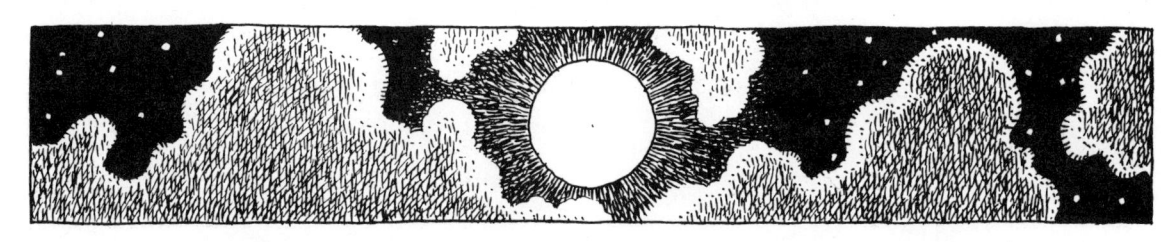

AUTUMN TARTS

3 to 4 large apples (winesap are excellent)
¾ cup red-currant jelly (use the kind made with honey, if possible)
⅔ cup water
2 to 4 drops natural food coloring (optional)
1 cup heavy cream
1 to 3 tablespoons honey, to taste
¼ teaspoon freshly grated nutmeg
Tart shells

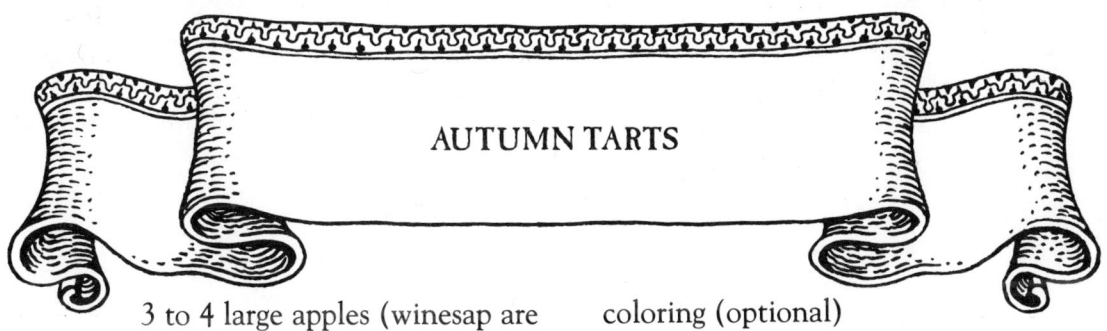

Peel and core the apples; cut them in half.

In a saucepan, melt the jelly with the water. Add the apples and simmer gently until they are tender but not mushy. If a red color is desired, add the drops of natural food coloring. Refrigerate. All this can be done ahead of time — up to a week if the shells are kept in a tightly closed container.

When ready to serve, whip the cream with the honey and nutmeg until the cream is stiff. Place a tart shell in a small bowl, fill it with cooked apples, top with whipped cream, then pour jelly and water sauce over the whipped cream. Serve at once.

Serves 6 to 8 humans or 8 elves.

Tart Shells

½ cup butter
1½ cups flour
¼ teaspoon salt
3 to 4 tablespoons cold water
¼ teaspoon cinnamon
⅛ teaspoon cloves
⅛ teaspoon allspice
1 tablespoon honey or sugar

Preheat oven to 400°.

Mix all the dry ingredients together.

Cut in the shortening until the mixture resembles coarse meal. Add the water a tablespoon at a time, mixing and forming a ball of dough. As you add the water, add the honey.

Let the dough rest for a few minutes. Roll it out very thin and shape it over tart pans.

Bake at 400° for 10 to 15 minutes, until light brown.

Makes 6 to 8 shells, depending on the size of the pans.

The very long and formal
courtship of betrothed elves
requires that certain rituals be performed, not
only by the couple, but also by their two families. Even
though the elf community is close-knit and the couple probably
have been friends since childhood, the elves feel that these
ceremonies develop a different and unique relationship between them.
    The courtship of Reena and Raoul is a classic example. Besides
the usual visits, meals, and gift giving between the two families, Raoul had his
companions periodically tell Reena and her family about his abilities and
accomplishments. In song and poetic recitation they recounted his heroic feats, such
as the time he saved the great elks from destruction by the gnomes, or praise his
markmanship. Raoul presented Reena with gifts he made for her, such as jewelry and
elaborate combs carved from special woods or shells. He always brought plants or flowers
that he had raised. Reena in turn designed garments for him, invented wonderful games
for them to play, made special quills for his arrows, and prepared her Fruit Yummy for him
(see page 108 for the recipe). Both wrote songs or poems and performed them at the
family gatherings. These activities and endless other duties were performed, until finally
the date for the uniting ceremony was set.
    At the ceremony they exchanged rings of their own making. Since uniting
always takes place during some spectacular celestial event, their ceremony took place
during a period of shooting stars. And as is the way with all events of any
importance, the celebration was time to culminate at the moment of the
celestial happening — in this case, the shooting stars.
    The dish called Tira's Snow was invented by Timmekin as a
present to her at their uniting ceremony. It is now the custom to
serve it at all uniting ceremonies as part of
the ritual. The snow is very lemony
and is best served with fresh
crushed raspberries, but
any berry is good.

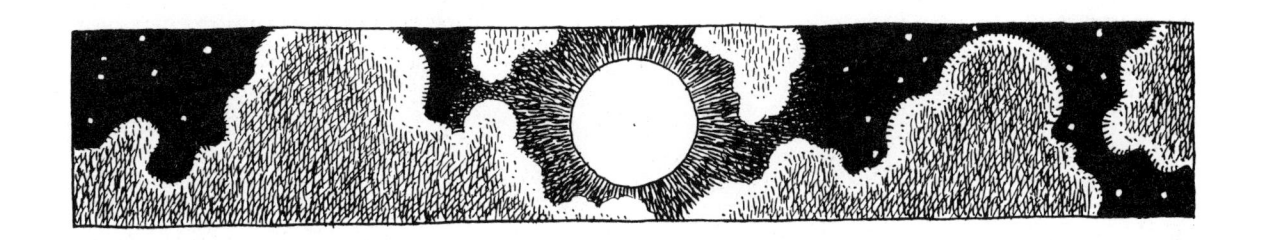

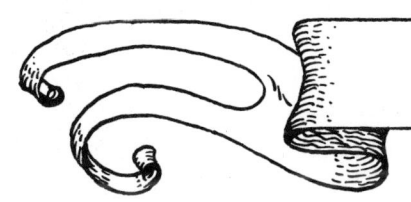

TIRA'S SNOW

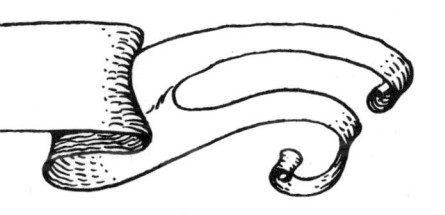

1 package gelatin
¼ cup cold water
¾ cup boiling water
½ cup Tupelo honey
Pinch of sea salt
⅓ cup lemon or ¼ cup lime juice
2¼ teaspoons grated lemon rind or 1½ teaspoons lime rind
2 egg whites
2 tablespoons honey or raw sugar
Strawberries, peaches, raspberries (optional)
Vanilla cream

Soften the gelatin in the cold water. In a bowl add the softened gelatin to the boiling water, Tupelo honey, salt, lemon juice, and rind. Stir until gelatin is completely dissolved. Cool until slightly thickened.

When gelatin has reached this stage, beat the egg whites until they form soft peaks. Add 2 tablespoons honey or sugar and beat the whites again until they hold a stiff peak. Fold in the lemon gelatin. Pour into a 6-cup mold. Chill until set. Unmold. Serve with vanilla cream, strawberries, peaches or raspberries.

Serves 4 humans or 8 elves.

Vanilla Cream

1 cup heavy cream
1 teaspoon vanilla
2 tablespoons honey

Stir all the ingredients together thoroughly.

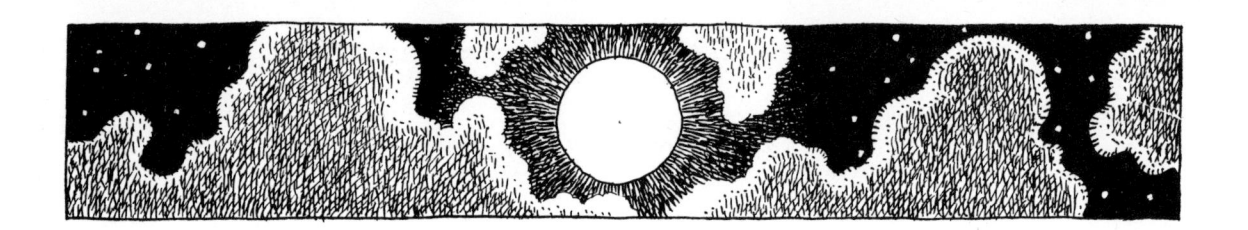

The fairy queen, Aureena, is a familiar sight in the elf city. Not only does she not have trouble finding the invisible Elvinor, but, more important, she visits with the elf children. Primarily Aureena acts as their protectress — a fairy godmother so to speak.

On each infant she bestows gifts. Later she offers advice when they come to her with their small problems. When they are fully grown, their fairy godmother will attend their uniting day and the birth of their children. And if they are chosen to be rulers, she will be present at their coronation.

Aureena is always the bearer of little gifts at these special occasions, but when Timmekin and Tira were crowned prince and princess, they gave presents to Aureena. She, in turn, brought a special dessert for the coronation feast, which has now become the traditional dessert.

THE FAIRY QUEEN'S PIE

1½ tablespoons gelatin
1 cup water
1 pint finest-quality vanilla ice cream (softened)
2 cups pureed cantaloupe (approximately ½ a large cantaloupe)
1 cup whipping cream (optional)
1 9-inch baked and cooled pie shell

Remove the ice cream from the freezer to soften it. Puree the cantaloupe in a blender or food processor.

In a large saucepan over low heat, dissolve the gelatin in the water. Stir until the gelatin is completely dissolved. Remove the pan from the heat.

Add the softened vanilla ice cream and the pureed cantaloupe to the gelatin and mix thoroughly and vigorously. The gelatin will begin to set almost immediately.

Pour the mixture into a cooled pie crust and refrigerate until ready to serve.

Sweetened whipped cream can be used to frost the pie. The top can be decorated with sliced strawberries and sliced melon.

Serves 6 to 8 humans or 12 to 14 elves.

An adventure, particularly for a band of young elves, does not mean doing only good deeds. Occasionally they will perform a deed or two that is *too* good. This is particularly true if they are near the Swamp of Mog, the domain of the witch Zormena. The hag prefers to keep her land overgrown and full of the stench of trees and plants rotting in the stagnant waters. Her skull-shaped castle scares all who approach. But to the carefree elfin youths, Zormena's place represents the ultimate challenge.

Working only when she is away — Zormena sometimes visits the goblins, and even the evil ice fairies are graced by her presence — the elf band silently and invisibly do their mischief, planting sweet-smelling flowers and cleaning up the murky waters. When she returns and discovers her land a beauty spot, the witch rages and promises herself revenge against the elves. But she is always thwarted, for her powers are limited. Then, Zormena must work for weeks using her evil spells to bring her domain back to its ugly best.

After such a triumph the elf band celebrates with a feast. They prepare crackers and dip, cheese puffs, carrots, and Triumph Pie for dessert.

TRIUMPH PIE

1 cup honey
2 tablespoons gelatin
½ cup water
6 eggs, separated
¼ to ½ teaspoon mace
1 teaspoon allspice
½ to 1 teaspoon cinnamon
¼ teaspoon freshly grated nutmeg
2½ cups cooked and mashed butternut squash (1 medium squash)
1 cup whipping cream
2 9-inch baked and cooled pie shells (page 21)

In a saucepan over low heat, dissolve the honey and the gelatin in the water, stirring continually.

In a bowl beat the egg yolks with an electric mixer or by hand until they are lemon-colored and thick. Add the spices and cooked squash. Mix in the honey-gelatin mixture. Place the squash mixture in the refrigerator until it is just beginning to set but is still slightly runny.

Beat the whipping cream until it forms stiff peaks. Fold the cream gently into the squash mixture. Spoon it into the cooked and cooled pie shells. Refrigerate until set. Keep in refrigerator until ready to serve.

Each pie makes 8 to 12 human servings or 16 elf servings.

VARIATIONS: The squash-cream mixture may be spooned into parfait glasses and layered with crushed ginger cookies or any type of cookie you prefer.

To accompany their snacks, elves usually have a milk beverage. Berry Drink is filling and very refreshing, especially for the elf children. Human children like it, too.

BERRY DRINK

1 teaspoon oil	½ teaspoon vanilla
¾ cup milk powder (whole, non-instant)	1 teaspoon honey
	½ cup strawberries
1½ cups water	1 cup ice cubes

or

2 cups milk	1 teaspoon vanilla
2 teaspoons soy powder	1 teaspoon honey
½ cup strawberries	3 to 4 ice cubes

Mix all the ingredients in a blender and serve at once.

Serves 2 humans or 4 elves.

The elves come in contact with all those who live in Zir. To some — like the clumsy trolls — they remain a mystery, only secretly performing their good deeds. To others, the elves are part of their lives. And to those unpleasant creatures — like the witch of the swamp — they are a nuisance. Yet without them, Zir and its inhabitants would suffer from neglect. For the elves' adventurous existence is filled with a service to life.

THE TROLLS

Fire! Fire!
Eye of fire
Hits the earth and cracks the sky.

Thunder! Thunder!
Rolling thunder
Hurts the ear but not the eye!

R aucous chantings and laughter echo again through the canyons of Gorak. It is the noise of the trolls, accompaniment for the lumbering band returning from their scavenging mission laden with supplies. For the subbornly independent trolls, any group undertaking presents the possibility of a fracas — either everyone wants to participate or no one will volunteer. More often than not the issue is settled by a battle of brawn. Remarkably, this particular trip ended successfully due to the efforts of the mulish and domineering Scug. Under his dogged control, the band snatched a bootle — a whole deer that had been shot just north of the canyons by a group of humans. The trolls got to the kill before the hunters and miraculously escaped without any reprisal. Now nearing home, each had begun chanting his own monotonous song, until Scug finally forced them to chant the same words.

 Owing to their antisocial nature, trolls only grudgingly organize themselves into rough communities of loosely linked individuals. The primitive huts and natural caves they call home are clustered together for protection, although each individual would prefer total isolation to the burden of ignoring his neighbor day after day.

 To be troll-like is to be in a bad mood generally, and you can be sure that a surly troll exterior hides an equally surly soul. After all, if day-to-day life is tough enough when one is slow, clumsly, and somewhat lazy, it becomes unbearable when when one lives in inhospitable canyons where the weather is either oppressively hot or windswept and cold. The trolls feel they owe it to themselves to be as unpleasant as possible to one another and to anyone else who crosses their path.

 While trolls are not basically foolhardy creatures, some have on occasion been lead astray to Rooma the witch, the ice fairies, or the black elves. These elves had hoped to keep mesmerized trolls as slaves, but even the strongest spells cast on the stubborn, fiercely independent captives could not penetrate their thick hides for long. The trolls soon escaped, free to go along their unmerry way, creating havoc (usually more for themselves than for others) along the way.

 In front of each hut or cave the trolls make their individual cook fires, and over every fire hangs a black, resinous pot in which practically everything is cooked. For breakfast trolls usually eat warmed leftovers from the night before. If every morsel of the evening meal has been devoured, something new is caught, cut, or stolen, thrown into the pot, and hastily cooked. This concoction constitutes the day's breakfast, lunch, and, they hope, dinner.

 The trolls' lack of interest in meal preparation does not mean that they are not interested in eating. As a matter of fact, these creatures not only love to eat but demand that the meal taste good, despite their unwillingness to cook it. The trolls feel that if a dish tastes good at breakfast it will taste just as good for their other meals throughout the day. After all, why be bothered cooking three times when once will do?

Since cauldron duty usually falls to the unfortunate troll who awakens first, they sleep as late as possible or at least keep their eyes closed until an unlucky compatriot's growling stomach forces him or her up. If a troll is living alone he will try to mooch first from relatives, then from anybody who happens to have a simmering meal. But trolls aren't known for their hospitality, and inevitably the single troll will have to start a fire and cook. Rule of thumb: Any troll who does the cooking is the most unpleasant troll for that entire day and should best be avoided.

The troll instinct for solitary living, or troll intolerance for the communal life, has brought about some rather peculiar mating rituals. Uniting with a partner is postponed as long as possible, often practically until old age; needless to say, very few offspring result. However, once united the couple is fiercely loyal, even if not very affectionate. Their relationship is based on toleration rather than admiration. Of course there is always a rare exception of a troll family that is more than civil to each other, but this behavior is viewed by the other villagers as strange, weird, and very untroll-like.

The ripening of the mugglevate fruit marks the beginning of troll courting season, although any traditional mating practices are subject to total cancellation if no troll seems interested that year. The mugglevate, a troll favorite, is a biannual fruit resembling our yarrow. Instead of flowers it bears orange berries that taste something like our blueberries. To the trolls it makes no difference whether male or female is the agressor, just so someone finally initiates courtship. The presentation of three sprigs of perfectly ripened mugglevate fruit constitutes the first formal approach to the intended — no other fruit will do.

In years when interest is high, trolls with mugglevate clutched firmly in their fists can be seen lumbering throughout the canyons. Each has already spent the most irritating years of life deciding on a partner, and now action can be taken. He or she will arrive at the "beloved's" doorway with fruit in hand. The door is opened, the fruit graciously accepted, and the suitor is left standing on the doorstep in anticipation of a response. The suitor needn't wait long, for soon an answer is delivered — a mud pie to the face or some mouldy stew to the head are sure signs that the intended has received the mugglevate and does not intend to reject the suitor completely. The pursuer will try again. An understanding has been reached if the next gift is returned in a torrent of dirty water. On an "off" day, the intended may pummel the wooer with pebbles or rocks, the size of the rocks being directly proportional to how "off" the quarry may be. Usually the fifth attempt will make the determination.

    Occasionally, on the first day of courting season, two intendeds may meet face to face, each holding their mugglevate, each in route through the canyon to the other's doorstep. Startled trolls are erratic trolls, and one of two things can occur. Either they will both turn and bolt to their respective homes, thus delaying courtship indefinitely while each waits for the other to make the first move, or one troll will run away and the other will follow, making for a uniquely brief and placid courtship.

    Trolls are known to be persistent suitors who eventually will win out even in the face of great adversity — and little can produce as great adversity as other trolls!

    A wedding ceremony takes place when five or more couples have squabbled, gnashed, and glared their way into commitment. Traditionally the ceremony is performed by the oldest married troll couple, but Alzar is always present and ready to end the festivities with a small light show.

    One of the trolls' favorite meats, liver, is always served at wedding feasts. Try this wedding stew on some of the non-liver-lovers in your household — they might change their minds.

WEDDING STEW

1 pound calves' or beef liver, sliced and floured
1 large onion, sliced thin (2½ cups)
⅓ green pepper, sliced in strips
3 to 3½ cups sliced potatoes
1 pound carrots
½ teaspoon salt
⅛ teaspoon pepper
Bacon fat
⅓ cup catsup
⅔ cup water

Preheat oven to 350°.

Brown the liver in the bacon fat. In a 2-quart oven casserole, layer the liver, onions, green peppers, potatoes and carrots. Salt and pepper each layer to taste. Blend the catsup and water together, and pour this mixture over the layered ingredients. Bake, covered, for 40 to 50 minutes.

Serves 4 to 6 humans or 2 wedded trolls.

Babies are very special to trolls, and the birth of a troll is cause for great celebration. Troll children are petted, hugged, kissed, and passed from troll to troll for cradling. But the moment they reach adolescence, mutual hostility between the adults and children develops. Their feelings are tempered into toleration as the children reach adulthood.

Everyone, even the most secluded troll, will come out to welcome a newborn. The villagers contribute to the celebration by bringing the new mother this hearty stew.

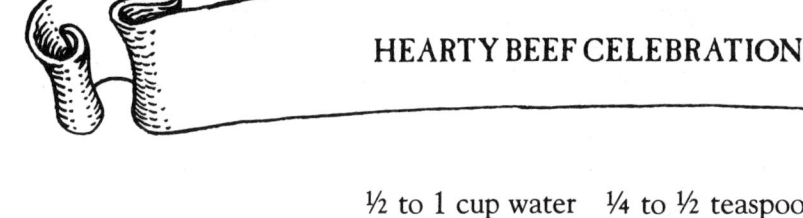

HEARTY BEEF CELEBRATION

½ to 1 cup water
3 pounds beef, cut into 2-inch cubes
2 pounds mushrooms
16 pearl onions
1 bay leaf
¼ to ½ teaspoon ground marjoram
¼ to ½ teaspoon ground thyme
12 ounces of beer (all natural if possible)
1 to 2 tablespoons oil
Salt
Freshly ground pepper

Preheat oven to 325°.

Wash mushrooms; trim bottoms of stems, leaving mushrooms whole. Peel onions. Brown cubed beef in oil in a Dutch oven, then remove and set aside.

Sauté the onions and mushrooms for one to 2 minutes in remaining oil. Return meat and add herbs, beer, and ½ cup water. Bake in oven for one hour. Check liquid level and add salt and freshly ground pepper to taste, then return to oven for 1 to 1½ hours. Serve over noodles or rice.

Serves 8 to 10 humans or 4 trolls — if they are not very hungry.

It is only logical that if a very large, clumsy, lazy, troll were to have a pet, he would choose an equally large animal that could fend for itself in the wake of its master's gracelessness and belligerence. Logic, unfortunately, does not hold with the trolls. Troll pets are small, fragile creatures kept locked in crude cages. They are carried around by their owners for companionship or display.

Yarg, a middle-aged unusually mellow female, has remained

petless for years because of her fellow trolls' "borrowing" of whatever beings she caught. So naturally, when she spied Petrie, a pixie, the desperate troll decided that she had finally found her one, true pet. Unbelievably, the cumbersom Yarg caught her! Yarg herself was so astonished at her all-thumbs success that she nearly lost her prize. But Petrie has been so enchanted by a perfect acorn she'd found that she had been trapped as much by her preoccupation as by Yarg's pudgy fingers.

    Yarg kept the pixie for some time before she began trusting the clever Petrie. Late one morning, Yarg, having inadvertently risen early, found that she was saddled with the chore of cooking. It threw her into a horrible frame of mind. Petrie siezed the opportunity to suggest that she, Petrie, do the cooking and teach Yarg a new, simple recipe. Yarg, anxious to escape responsibility, enthusiastically agreed. The freed pixie prepared mountains of food, and the gluttonous trolls descended upon it with greedy mouths and grabbing hands. While her captor was completely engrossed in getting her share of the real, the sly Petrie escaped.

    Yarg was again without a pet, but at least she knew how to prepare a meal.

PETRIE'S STEW

1 pound ground chuck	1 pound fresh string beans
¾ cup chopped onion	1 tablespoon oil
1 large clove garlic	10 grinds pepper (¼ teaspoon)
1 cup tomato puree	1 teaspoon salt
¾ cup water	2 eggs, beaten

In a skillet, sauté onion and garlic in oil over medium heat until onions are translucent. Crumble in the meat and brown. Add the string beans, water, tomato puree, salt, and pepper. Cook, covered, until green beans are tender-crisp and bright green in color. Pour beaten eggs over all and continue cooking until eggs are set. Stir only 2 or 3 times, leaving the eggs in several large portions. Serve immediately.

Serves 4 to 5 humans or one troll.

Of the two sexes, female trolls appear to be slightly smarter and somewhat less obstinate than their male counterparts. A female has the knack of getting her mate, if she has one, or her children to perform certain chores without resorting to excessive violence. Narb, for example, keeps a small garden that she protects against poachers with tooth and club. Her indentured (or indented, if she chooses to use the club) family help cultivate her vegetables and herbs. Since a variety of wild birds are native to the canyons, now and again they, too, end up in the cooking pot. Narb uses this recipe when someone has snared her a bird or two.

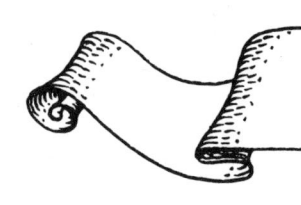

CHICKEN & POTATOES

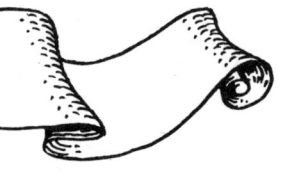

1 3-pound chicken, cut into serving pieces.	1 medium onion, diced
Salt and pepper to taste	½ teaspoon ground coriander
1 cup flour	½ teaspoon oregano
	¼ teaspoon thyme

¼ cup oil
3 or 4 large potatoes, diced small
10 to 12 mushrooms, sliced
1 large carrot, cut into rounds
1 stalk celery, coarsely chopped
½ medium green pepper, coarsely chopped (trolls like hot ones)
½ bay leaf
1 cup canned tomato puree or ½ cup fresh tomato puree and ½ cup water
1½ to 2 cups water, as needed to keep stew moist

Cut the chicken (turkey pieces or 2½ pounds of cubed beef can be substituted for chicken) into serving pieces and season with salt and pepper. Dredge in flour to coat, then sauté over medium-high heat until chicken pieces are brown. Remove them from the pan and set aside.

In the same pan sauté the onions until they are limp, then add diced potatoes and continue to sauté until potatoes are well coated with oil and some are beginning to brown. Add the carrots and green pepper to coat with oil, then stir in mushrooms.

Return the chicken to the pan, pour in tomato puree and water, and add coriander, oregano, thyme, and bay leaf. Bring to a boil, then lower the heat and simmer, covered, for 40 minutes or until chicken is tender. This stew will make its own gravy.

Serves 6 humans or one troll.

Troll clothing is made from nearly anything dragged home from scavenging trips. Skins and furs, cold-weather wear, are the least objectionable of their fashions. Troll cloth is crudely woven from leaves, twigs, feathers, and even the hair of a fellow troll taken unaware. A typical piece will be clotted with dangling goldenwood leaves and silkworm cocoons and even fringed with poisonous vines, to which the trolls are completely impervious. Not much penetrates their tough skin. The look can be interesting, but the smell can be devastating to others, a side effect the trolls welcome. Both male and female trolls weave, and they pride themselves on the variations, textures, and quality of their cloth.

To celebrate the completion of a large piece of their crude looms, the female will prepare this troll favorite.

COVERED APPLES

4 apples, peeled and cored
3 tablespoons flour
½ teaspoon cinnamon
¼ teaspoon cloves
¼ teaspoon allspice
⅓ to ½ cup honey, maple syrup, brown sugar, or turbinado sugar
4 tablespoons butter
1 egg plus 1 teaspoon water

Preheat oven to 350°.

Mix the flour, cinnamon, cloves, allspice and sweetener together. Place an apple in center of each square of dough.

Divide flour-sweetener mixture into 4 equal parts and spoon over apples and top each with one tablespoon butter. Overlap dough around apple to cover. With any extra pieces, cut out leaf shapes and decorate the surface.

Place in baking pan. Beat the egg with water and brush over the surface of dough to glaze. Bake for 40 minutes.

Can be served with cream.

Four apples serve one troll if he or she can keep the others away.

Dough

½ cup mashed cooked sweet potatoes or yams
1 egg
½ cup butter
1½ cup flour (unbleached special blend or whole-wheat)
Pinch of salt

Mix the flour and the salt together. Cut in butter with two knives or pastry blender until mixture resembles coarse meal. Mix mashed sweet potatoes and egg together and then add to flour mixture. Dough will be soft. Divide into 4 parts and roll out into squares about ⅜-inch thick. Trim if necessary.

Trolls are very talented mimics. They are particularly skilled at bird calls, so much so that those natural sounds have become part of the trolls' music. Surrounded by thumping drums and clattering sticks, an independent troll can show off his particular talents, provided his fellow trolls will allow it.

Refreshments are usually served after one of these musical evenings. The unlucky troll who must prepare the desserts for the day whips up something simple.

APPLE CRUST

8 large apples, sliced in 8ths
1¼ teaspoon nutmeg
¼ cup brown sugar or 2 tablespoons honey
1 cup unbleached flour
¾ cup brown sugar or ⅓ cup honey
1 tablespoon baking powder
¼ teaspoon salt
1¾ cups cream

Preheat oven to 400°.

Mix the apples, nutmeg, and brown sugar together. Layer in a baking dish and set aside.

Mix batter by stirring together the remaining ingredients with the cream.

Pour batter over apple mixture. Bake for about 30 minutes, until top is browned. Serve warm, plain or with whipped cream.

Serves 8 to 10 humans or 4 musical trolls.

The community of humans in the northern village of Ohnam were in an uproar about the scavenging bands of trolls. Their animals weren't safe; their crops weren't safe; why, even the weeds that grew along their roads were woven into troll cloth before they could be pulled by the humans. With weapons in hand, the men marched off to teach the trolls a lesson.

With the vigilantes marched Pook Oakelbuck, a renegade

dwarf. Pook, having no real quarrel with either the men, or the trolls, marched only to see if he could have some fun at either party's expense. As a prankster, he was also at an advantage, since, through the power of a magical hat, he had deviously acquired from an ancient magician, Pook marched invisibly.

    The men arrived at the end of the canyons and shouted their challenge to the trolls. The men were ready to attack, when suddenly Pook materialized, standing fifteen formidable feet tall between the two motley groups. The frenzied men, unable to stop after running full tilt down the steep canyonside, began attacking Pook. He disappeared. They, along with the trolls, who were haphazardly trying to defend themselves, were stunned and afraid. Pook appeared again, this time even larger, and with a proposal of peace for both sides. Both terrified bands listened and took heed.

    Pook proposed an annual contest between the trolls and the men with a hefty prize — there had to be a prize or no self-respecting troll would participate — awarded to the winner. If the trolls won they would be free to plunder prescribed fields once a month, with the understanding that they would loot no other place around the northern village. If the men won, however, ten trolls would report to the human village and work the fields for one week per month, all year.

    The competition game devised by Pook was a cross between football and armed combat. Sticks no longer than four feet and no weapon larger than three inches in diameter would be allowed. Plain shields were permitted. A ball was made from a very large rock covered with fur and tied with leather. The object of the game was to move the ball, using the allowed weapons plus hands, heads, teeth, and other natural defense systems, to a goal area across the field. Each team was allowed only fifteen players on the field at a time — but replacements for the wounded and bedraggled were unlimited. There would be no time limitations — the first team to reach 100 points would win.

    The not-too-bright, lazy, clumsy trolls instantly comprehended that losing meant *work*. They learned the rules to the game quickly and never worked so hard winning that first game. They have lost in other years, but not very many times.

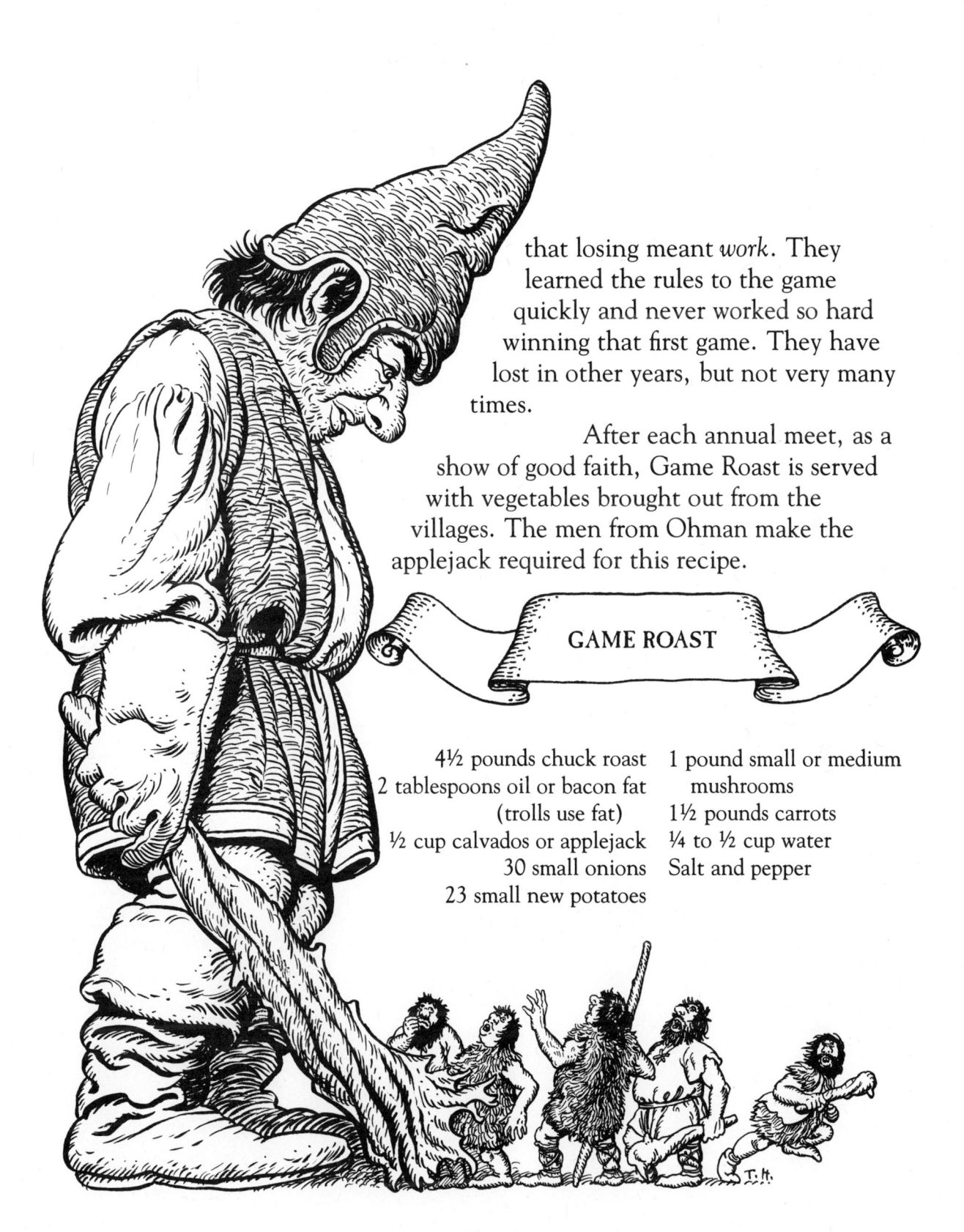

After each annual meet, as a show of good faith, Game Roast is served with vegetables brought out from the villages. The men from Ohman make the applejack required for this recipe.

GAME ROAST

4½ pounds chuck roast
2 tablespoons oil or bacon fat (trolls use fat)
½ cup calvados or applejack
30 small onions
23 small new potatoes
1 pound small or medium mushrooms
1½ pounds carrots
¼ to ½ cup water
Salt and pepper

Clean mushrooms and leave whole, but trim off the bottom of the stem. Scrub carrots and cut into large pieces. Peel onions and wash potatoes. Set all vegetables aside.

In a large, heavy Dutch oven, heat oil and brown the roast on all sides at a high temperature. Remove the meat. Add all vegetables and stir-fry them for one to 2 minutes, then remove them and set them aside again. Return meat to pan and add calavados; bring to a boil, remove from heat and add vegetables, water, and salt and pepper to taste. Cover and simmer over low heat until tender, about one to 1½ hours, and baste with juices frequently.

Serves 8 to 10 humans or 4 troll game players.

Pook became a fixture in the canyons, at least when the erratic weather suited him. Because of his dwarfish instincts he was intrigued by all the colored stones that lined the canyon floor — stones that held little interest for the trolls, unless some unsuspecting creature wandered within striking distance. One day he enlisted some trolls' aid in completing a minor chore, promising great gifts in return. When, some days later, the grumpy trolls began demanding payment for their halfhearted efforts, Pook gathered a small basket full of rocks and disappeared. The trolls were outraged. Pook finally turned up, a week later, to face an angry, armed mob of wronged trolls ready to exact the cost of their labor with Pook's flesh. Pook responded to the commotion by pointing skyward — where a flying horse appeared, circled gracefully, then landed in the canyon. Its packs were laden with exotic breads and ground grains, all unfamiliar to the astounded trolls. Somehow it was all divided and the trolls ate more than their fill.

The next day Pook began teaching the trolls to make the Flat Bread they so enjoyed. Here's the recipe just as he gave it to the trolls. He told them they would need:

> 1 large bowl of wood or clay
>   (glass or stainless ok, too)
> 2 scoops of dark flour
>   (2 cups of whole-wheat flour)
> 1 scoop of light flour
>   (1 cup unbleached or special-mixture flour)

2 scoops of white powder
  (2 teaspoons of baking powder)
2 spoons salt
  (2 teaspoons salt)
1 small scoop of fat
  (approximately ⅔ cup lard)
1 gourd of hot water
  (½ cup very hot water)
Extra flour for working dough

With your hands, mix both flours, white powder (baking powder), and salt in the bowl until it takes on a uniform appearance and texture. Add the lard in pieces and work into the flour with your fingers. When it is properly mixed it will look like a coarse meal. To make sure enough lard has been incorporated in the dough, pick up some of the mixture in your hand and gently squeeze it in your palm. If the flour sticks together the fat content is sufficient. Do this several times, sampling all areas of the dough. Mix in hot water until dough forms a soft ball — it will stiffen as you work with it.

The male trolls especially enjoy the next step — kneading. Knead the dough for 20 to 25 minutes, then cover it with a clean cloth and let it rest at least 4 hours or overnight. To cook, shape into one-inch balls and roll out into 4- to 5-inch circles, each about ¼ inch thick. Cook on a hot, lightly greased griddle, turning as you would a pancake, until golden brown. Wrap in a towel to keep warm or serve at once.

Of course, trolls make gigantic circles of dough and cook them on hot stones. They eat their homemade bread with stews or slathered with honey, butter, or anything spreadable and tasty. Male trolls are expert at making and eating the flat bread introduced to them by Pook via the winged horse. It was later learned that the beautiful steed was a prized pet of the Amazons, who used the animal to expedite their trading of unusual stones for breads and grains.

When the awkward trolls learned to make bread they blundered into the discovery of noodles along the way. At first their noodles were thick, coarse, and bland, but with practice the trolls became very skilled at producing thin, light strands that would nearly melt in their mouths. They then began making this easy and delicious dish.

TROLL NOODLES

1 pound ground chuck
½ to ⅔ pounds thin spaghetti, broken in thirds
2 tablespoons oil
½ medium green pepper, chopped fine
¾ cups onions, chopped fine
1 clove, garlic, minced (optional)

1½ cups canned tomato sauce or puree or 3 cups fresh tomato puree
1 teaspoon salt
8 grinds pepper (about ⅛ teaspoon)
½ to 1 cup water or as needed (½ cup, if fresh tomato puree used)

Brown the broken spaghetti in oil and set aside. Mix salt into ground chuck and make meatballs one to 1½ inches in diameter. Set them in the bottom of an oiled stove-top casserole and cover them with a layer of the brown spaghetti. Mix peppers, onions, garlic, tomato sauce, and pepper together and pour over meatballs and spaghetti. Then pour water over all. Cook, covered, over low heat for 30 minutes without lifting lid. If, after 30 minutes, casserole seems dry, add some additional water. After checking, cook, covered, for 45 to 50 minutes or until spaghetti is tender. The spaghetti will have absorbed the liquids, and casserole will be moist but not watery. Troll noodles may also be cooked in the oven for one hour at 325°.

Hunting! Hunting!
Spearing! Spearing!
Game for humans,
Traps he sets for him, not I.

Quietly! Stealing!
Trapping game birds,
Trolls will play while humans cry.

Running! Running!
Escape! Escaping!
He calls us dumb,
But we spit in his eye!
Or at least we try!

THE FAIRIES

The signs in the sky are unmistakable. All of the inhabitants of Zir watch and wait, trembling with anticipation. The night heavens are bright with the usual diamond-like sparkle of the stars, but tonight something is different — for there against the black sky special lights twinkle, rarely seen beacons that signal to everyone in Zir that something fantastic is very, very near.

In the canyons of Gorak, the trolls hide themselves in terror. At Elvinor, the elves watch the sky, engaged in solemn celebration. High in his mountain home, Alzar the wizard gazes, entranced, at the night vision, anticipating the message that will soon be delivered to him. Tonight, just as surely as the miraculous stars always return, a new fairy princess will come to Zir.

In plain view of all the continent, yet totally unseen, the princess will arrive. Not even the fairies themselves quite understand the mysterious appearance of the new princess, yet they gather in the queen's garden to perform the secret ceremony necessary to invite her arrival. Large and small alike hover in a circle surrounding the queen, who presides over the solemnities from a throne wrapped with flowering vines. With their arms uplifted and fingers ever so slightly touching one another's, the fairies, as if with one voice, sing out an eerie but soothing tone. The lights in the sky begin to spin and the fairies song increases in intensity until the whirling lights move, converging into one blinding spiral, as if summoned by the sound toward the fairies below. The blazing aura approaches Zir, settling finally into the fairies' circle. A great flash and it is gone, but in its place stands the princess. Her features are childlike and innocent, yet she comes armed with the knowledge of the universe.

The fairies of Zir are diverse in type, size, and temperament. There are fairies as large as the average human, fairies that can hide in a flower, and fairies of every size in between. Some are innocent and virtuous, others corrupt to the core. But despite their differences in appearance and polarities in behavior, there is one thing characteristic of all fairies — they are all busybodies. Their desire to get involved in the lives of the inhabitants of Zir is uncontrollable, and their meddling can result in anything from a childish prank to an act of mercy, although corrupt fairies have been proved responsible for some real atrocities.

Apart from their interest in the personal affairs of those around them, fairies have an intricate society and communal life to which they are devoted. Each separate group of fairies is governed by a princess or lesser queen, but all pay allegience to Aureena, the fairy queen. Each type of fairy has its own purpose, and their services help either the community of fairies or other parts of Zir. Some assist in the pollination of flowers, while others preserve the especially perfect blooms that are worn like jewels by the rest of the fairies. Some weave a delicate gossamer cloth from cobwebs, milkweed-pod silk or old broken insect cocoons. Groups of larger fairies master the weather and oversee the efforts of their smaller sisters. Because the fairy world and its inhabitants evolved from nature, the fairies have a rare control over it — or at least a certain part of it.

This female society is totally vegetarian — in fact, fairies eat no animal products. They have attained such a state of magical perfection that the idea of consuming another being or any of its products is repugnant to them. Fairies, large or small, never consume a filling amount of food at one sitting. Instead, they eat many small meals a day to renew their energy — larger fairies nibble at six to eight meals during the day, while the small ones eat as many as twelve or sixteen times. They may serve only one or two types of food at each meal or they may have a variety on hand, but it is always served out in very tiny portions.

Many of our ancient human societies learned dietary secrets from the fairies simply because the fairies couldn't resist getting involved in the development of their civilizations. Traces of their influence are still apparent in twentieth-century human customs and similarities in daily menu still remain. They breakfast on a fruit drink or an airy shake. Later they break from their activities for a whole-grain cake or biscuit. Lunch may consist of salad, a touch of cooked greens and legumes, or soy with mullet. Teatime is always marked by the serving of weed tea and a sweet. Fruits may be stewed for dinner and tea is brewed with honey and lemon at bedtime.

Fairy cheese, a vegetable cheese made by the large fairies, has a flavor similar to goat-milk cheese, or cottage cheese, but its texture is smooth like that of cheddar or swiss.

Fairies flavor their cheeses with herbs or spices and use them in combination with vegetables, fruits, and grains. The best substitute available to humans for use in the fairies' favorite recipes is tofu, or bean curd. The two marinades that follow will impart the taste of herbed fairy cheese to tofu, which is available in most markets.

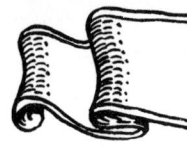

MARINADE I

1 teaspoon Vegex or 1 tablespoon vegetable soup concentrate
½ cup warm water
¼ teaspoon chervil
½ teaspoon taragon
1 tablespoon sauterne wine
1 tablespoon chives

Mix all ingredients together and marinate tofu from 1 to 3 hours or overnight. Tempeh, a soy product available at health-food stores, can be substituted ounce for ounce for tofu, but marinate tempeh overnight, as it does not take up the marinade as quickly.

The marinated tempeh or tofu can also be breaded or floured and sautéed in oil for a hot appetizer or side dish.

MARINADE II

½ teaspoon Vegex or ½ tablespoon dry vegetable soup concentrate
½ cup warm water
½ bay leaf
¼ teaspoon thyme
½ teaspoon savory
¼ teaspoon marjoram

Mix all ingredients together and marinate tofu at least 1 to 3 hours or overnight. Can also be used with tempeh, as in previous recipe.

The following sauce is a delightful accompaniment to the marinated and sautéed tofu.

SAUCE

1½ to 2 cups mushrooms
2 tablespoons butter or oil
1½ teaspoons each minced dried onion
tarragon and chives
Reserved Marinade I or II
1 to 1½ cups vegetable broth made with Vegex
1 teaspoon arrowroot mixed with 1 tablespoon water
2 tablespoons sauterne wine

In oil, sauté mushrooms and dried onion. Add wine, vegetable broth, and marinade. Bring to a boil, then reduce to a simmer before adding arrowroot-and-water mixture. *Do not boil.* Arrowroot makes a delicate sauce and it will thicken the hot liquid.

Serve over warm tofu or tempeh.

If a mischievous fairy can be annoying, a completely corrupt fairy can make mere misery seem like bliss. Therefore Fairy Queen Aureena sees to it that her good fairies protect the inhabitants of Zir from the menacing acts of the evil ones.

From the ice castle, the cold and calculating Queen Marzetta rules in Daln. Once an honored princess ruling over hundreds of fairies, her diplomatic expeditions frequently brought her to the ice land of Daln. There she fell under the influence of a cunning old hag who preyed on the young fairy's pride. Marzetta soon became arrogant and self-absorbed, disdaining all but her own group of ruthless followers who helped to bolster her vanity by undercutting all others renowned for beauty or power. Finally, when she challenged the very throne of Aureena, a confrontation between Marzetta and the other fairies came about; but the crone had done her work well and the proud princess refused to acknowledge the hierarchy of the fairy empire.

Marzetta and her followers flew to Daln in a fury. From her arctic kingdom she gives vent to her jealous rage against the creatures of Zir by using her power over the weather, stretching the bleak winter well into spring and sending the raw winds to destroy crops.

This corrupt band must constantly increase its supply of slaves to rule and abuse. Casting spells to capture the unsuspecting, they can turn a dwarf into a goblin or an elf into a gremlin. These unlucky creatures slowly lose all recollection of their lives before the transformation, but not even the strongest spell can eradicate their desire for freedom.

Aureena and the good fairies try to recover those bewitched by the evil Marzetta, but finding the antidote for each spell is nearly impossible since the Daln fairies constantly change them. But no sorcery is stronger than the charm of simple goodness, and often a whisper, or the singing of lovely songs, or eating a wholesome meal can make an enchanted dwarf himself again.

Here is one soup used by the fairies for such a purpose; you can use it to bring out the best in any mesmerized member of your family.

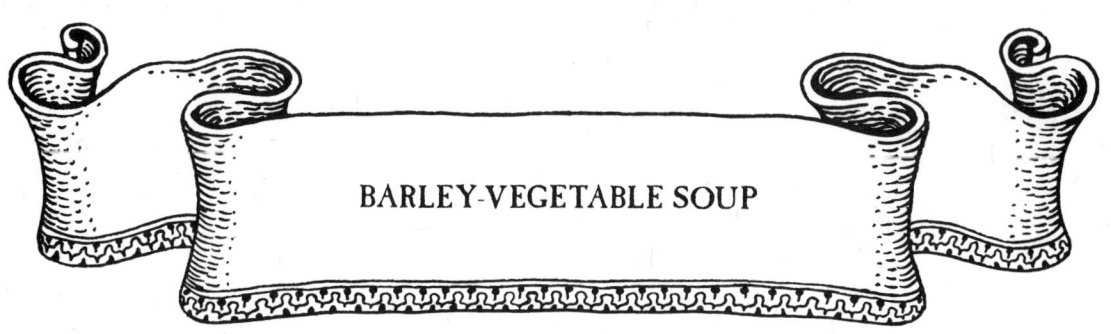

BARLEY-VEGETABLE SOUP

½ cup pearl barley
6 cups water
2 teaspoons sea salt
1⅔ cups chopped tomato
1 bay leaf
¼ teaspoon sage
½ teaspoon oregano

1½ teaspoons oil
1 onion, sliced
1 stalk celery, chopped
½ cup peas, fresh or frozen
2½ cups zucchini or yellow
  squash, coarsely chopped
¼ cup sliced mushrooms

Bring barley to a boil in water and salt; simmer 45 minutes or until soft. Add tomatoes, bay leaf, sage, and oregano. While mixture simmers, sauté onion and celery in oil. When the onion is translucent, add the peas, squash, and mushrooms. Sauté together for 3 minutes, then add to soup. Continue simmering for 10 minutes, then serve.

Serves 24 fairies or 8 humans.

With the endless variety and abundant growth of vegetation in Zir, the fairies have a splendid diet. One of its mainstays is salad, with or without dressing.

For a little fairy like Merria, a salad lunch may be best enjoyed with a picnic, usually spread on a large leaf or branch. She throws her colorful cloth over the branch and carefully sets out her plates or bowls—which are shells. Her thumbnail-size cups and saucers, a gift from a dwarf potter whom she helped by rescuing his children from a group of goblins sent by Marzetta, balance solidly on a wide knot of wood. While Merria waits for her guests, two more of her tiny kind, she unpacks their lunch of Field Salad with Lemon-Honey Drizzle.

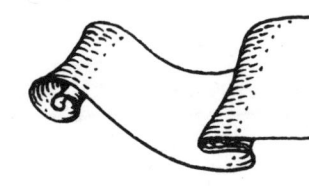

FIELD SALAD

4 carrots grated
3 stalks celery
1 cup alfalfa sprouts
Lemon Honey Drizzle (recipe follows)

Combine carrots, celery, and sprouts until well mixed. Pour Lemon Honey Drizzle over field salad and toss to coat.

Serves 4 humans, 4 large fairies, or a party of 20 of Merria's friends.

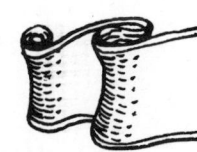

LEMON-HONEY DRIZZLE

Juice of 2 lemons
1 to 2 tablespoons honey
1/3 cup sunflower
Salt to taste

Mix ingredients together in blender or shaker jar.

Deep within her green kingdom, the fairy queen resides in her tree palace. The interwoven branches of living trees, as old as Zir itself, frame her splendid home, and vines of blooming lavender and white wildflowers form a living border around the grand gothic foyer and windows. Lace curtains spun by the most delicate fairies from flower petals and spider silk drape each portal. Every room is carpeted by bright green moss, and in the main hall a babbling brook gently chatters a soothing song. Entering nature's luxury brings a sense of peace and a feeling of total contentment to all who visit.

Here Aureena lives with her court, welcomes visitors and envoys, and entertains at high festivals. She even prepares some fairy specialties herself, including her own creation, Queen's Almond Loaf. It is always served as the main dish at the celebration of the northern lights.

QUEEN'S ALMOND LOAF

3½ cups kale, chopped
  (you can also use spinach or any leafy green vegetable)
3 to 4 tablespoons water
¼ cup oil
1 medium onion, finely chopped
3 tablespoons fresh parsley, finely chopped
¼ cup green peppers
1 clove garlic, finely chopped
1 rib celery, finely chopped
2 cups ground raw nuts (use almonds, pecans, cashews in any proportion; for example, 1 cup almonds, ¾ cup pecans, ¼ cup cashews)
1 cup dried whole-wheat bread crumbs
  (toast stale bread for a few minutes, then make crumbs in blender, food processor, or food mill)
½ cup toasted wheat germ
1 to 1½ teaspoon brewer's yeast
¼ to ⅓ cup catsup or chili sauce
1 tablespoon soy sauce
½ teaspoon oregano
½ teaspoon marjoram
¼ teaspoon thyme

Preheat oven to 350°.

Finely chop the green vegetables and steam them in the water. Cool and set aside. Sauté the chopped onion, parsley, peppers, garlic, and celery in the oil. For color you may use one red pepper or add some pimiento.

Mix the nuts and bread crumbs together, then add the wheat germ, yeast, catsup or chili, sauce and soy sauce. Sprinkle the herbs over the mixture. Add the sautéed greens and, using your hands, mix well, then form into a loaf shape. Place on a greased cookie sheet bake for 30 to 40 minutes.

Serves 20 large fairies, 100 small fairies, or 4 to 6 humans

Both of Merria's guests have brought her hostess gifts, as is the custom. Since they were invited for salad, each has brought a sampling of her own prized salad dressing and some special greens found only in the mountain of Thordarn, where the giants live.

Here is the secret recipe for a gift any hostess would love to receive.

TAHINI SALAD DRESSING

3 to 4 tablespoons tahini
½ teaspoon onion powder
1 tablespoon vinegar
½ cup water
½ teaspoon Vegesal
¼ teaspoon thyme
½ teaspoon marjoram

Combine all ingredients in blender or shake in covered jar. Serve with green or vegetable salad. If you add a little honey this will make an interesting dressing for fruit.

Visits to Elvinor are made by Queen Aureena and her devotees frequently, because Her Highness especially loves to play with and talk to the spirited elf children. The elves, however, rarely visit the fairy queen in return, since the palace is constantly abuzz with fairy visitors who come for advice, help, or relaxation. Of course, when the elves are invited they waste no time in packing up their belongings, their children, and gifts for Aureena and hurry off to that wonderful place. No one who has visited the fairy palace ever forgets the overwhelming feeling of peace found within its confines.

Knowing how the elves love to eat, Aureena serves a veritable banquet to greet the entourage from Elvinor. And the anticipation of one dish — Aureena's Vegetable Stroganoff — helps the elves through the last leg of their journey.

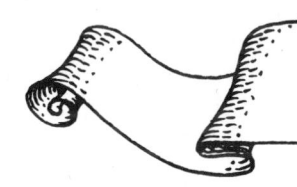

VEGETABLE STROGANOFF

½ pound tofu
¼ cup tamari
2 teaspoons Worcestershire Sauce
½ to 1 teaspoon garlic powder
1 tablespoon sherry
¼ cup water
¼ cup celery, sliced thinly
¼ cup carrots, sliced into thin rounds
3 cups fresh mushrooms, sliced
½ cup minced onion or scallion
¼ teaspoon marjoram
¼ teaspoon basil
¼ teaspoon salt
¼ teaspoon dill weed
4 to 6 grinds pepper (⅛ teaspoon)
3 tablespoons sauterne, or other white wine, vegetable broth, or apple juice
½ cup yogurt or sour cream
Pinch of nutmeg
½ bay leaf (optional)
2 to 4 tablespoons oil

Cut tofu into ⅜-inch slices. Combine next five ingredients and marinate tofu for 1 to 2 hours.

In a deep skillet, sauté the onions or scallions in oil until they are translucent. Add sliced mushrooms and sauté until mushrooms are tender. Stir in marjoram, dill weed, basil, salt, pepper, and white wine, vegetable broth, or juice. Add bay leaf, if desired.

When this mixture is simmering, add tofu and marinade. Bring to a boil, lower heat, and mix in yogurt and nutmeg.

Fairies eat no animal products, and if you avoid them, too, substitute soy yogurt and soy sour cream for the dairy ingredients in this recipe. Vegetarians may do the same, or omit the products altogether. Although the tart stroganoff taste produced by the yogurt or sour cream will be absent, the dish will be savory.

Though most fairies — even the most meddlesome — consider their duties a pleasure rather than a chore, they deserve a day to play, sing, and relax with their co-workers. So Aureena sets aside a special day for the fairies' annual picnic, and since one of the last-minute details is to manipulate the weather, it is always a glorious day with clear blue skies and plenty of sun.

Many of the same activities enjoyed by human children — relays, games, and such — have been tailored to the fairies' unique talents. It is not unusual, then, that most of the revelers at the annual picnic participate in the flying races. There are many categories in which to compete, such as endurance flying, obstacle course, and flying in circles without getting dizzy. Each size fairy competes within her own group, then finalists of all sizes vie for the grand championship on a course set by the queen; the race is timed by several impartial judges. The winner of the day receives a special jeweled crown and the best meal available in the kingdom to be prepared by the cook of her choice.

A tiny dew fairy was the champion four years in a row. Her choice each time was Squash à la Queen, a stuffed squash dish prepared by Aureena.

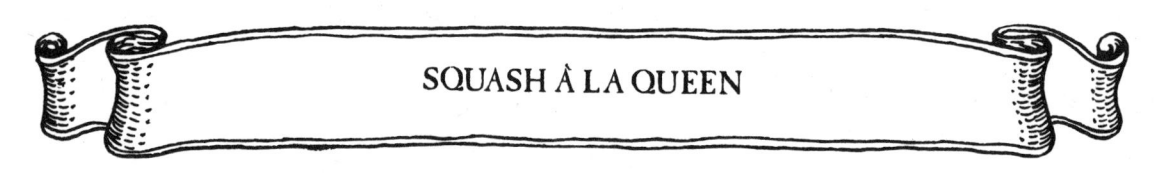

SQUASH À LA QUEEN

2 crooked neck or yellow squash
1 large onion
1 stalk celery
½ green pepper
1 carrot
1 clove garlic
¼ teaspoon thyme
½ teaspoon rosemary
¾ teaspoon dill
½ teaspoon salt
4 grinds pepper
2 shredded-wheat biscuits, crumbled

3 tablespoons oil
¼ teaspoon savory
Ground almonds, filberts, or cheese for topping

Preheat oven to 375°.

Cut squash in half lengthwise. Scoop out meat, leaving only a thin shell. Using a processor fitted with a metal blade, chop finely the onion, celery, green pepper, carrot, garlic and squash meat. Sauté chopped vegetables in oil with savory, thyme, rosemary, dill, salt, and pepper until most of the moisture has evaporated. Add crumbled shredded wheat and combine well.

Stuff each squash shell with mixture, top with ground nuts, and dot with butter or grated cheese. Bake for 15 to 20 minutes.

Serves 4 humans.

One of the most difficult and most rewarding tasks is the responsibility of the water fairies. They care for all streams and lakes in Zir. Every fish, animal, and insect, every bit of mossy vegetation that finds a secure home in or near the water, receives the tender care of these sprites. With all this work to do, the water fairies have little chance to interact with Zir's other inhabitants, except when visitors come to the waterways. Yet even welcomed guests take care not to pollute the area; the wrath of the water fairies can make any transgressor forever regret careless actions.

Lileen makes her home in a water lily, as do so many of her friends, but the fairies also live in hanging homes high up in the tree branches. They receive frequent visits from Aureena. The queen appreciates how difficult the work of the water fairies is, and she rewards her industrious subjects with gifts of clothes, food, or assistance. Sometimes the tiny guardians of the waterways need larger fairies to help with unwieldy projects.

One of the dishes frequently brought to the water fairies by Aureena is a mixed vegetable casserole with a tomato sauce accompaniment.

TOMATO SAUCE

1 tablespoon olive oil
1 tablespoon safflower oil
2 tablespoons tamari
¾ teaspoon ground ginger
⅔ cup pear juice
½ teaspoon ground cumin
½ teaspoon ground coriander
¼ teaspoon ground cardamom
¼ teaspoon dill seed
½ teaspoon celery seed
1 tablespoon minced onions (optional)
4 cups fresh tomato puree
2 tablespoons tomato paste
½ unpeeled apple, finely chopped
⅛ cantaloupe or musk melon, peeled and finely chopped
2 tablespoons raisins
¼ cup sunflower seeds
2 tablespoons sesame seeds
1 teaspoon cider vinegar

Place ingredients into a large pot in the order given and simmer on low heat for 45 minutes to an hour.

Tomato Sauce is delicious over whole-wheat pasta, Jerusalem artichoke pasta, spaghetti squash, or Vegetables à la Water Fairies (recipe follows)

VEGETABLES À LA WATER FAIRIES

1 tablespoon oil
1 pound string beans
About 2 small zucchini, sliced (3 cups)
About 2 small yellow squash, sliced (4 cups)
1 medium eggplant cut in large chunks
1 green pepper, chopped (1 cup)
½ pound mushrooms, cut in halves
½ medium onion thinly sliced (optional)
½ pound tofu, plain or marinated (page 140)
bread crumbs or flour for coating
¼ cup oil
¼ cup oil
Tomato Sauce (recipe above)

Sauté all the vegetables in 1 tablespoon oil for 3 minutes, then cover and steam over low heat until tender.

Slice marinated or plain tofu in slices ¼ to ⅜ inch thick. Dip in bread crumbs or wheat flour and sauté in ¼ cup oil. Drain and set aside.

To serve, place tofu on a plate, surround it with vegetables, and cover with prepared tomato sauce.

This coconut dish is one of Aureena's favorites. It can be allowed to set in a decorative mold and served with a sauce of fruit puree, or it can be cubed and mixed into a fruit salad.

QUEEN'S MOLDED COCONUT

1 coconut
1½ cups hot water
2 tablespoons agar-agar
2 cups water
¾ teaspoon vanilla extract
¼ teaspoon almond extract
4 tablespoons strawberry honey

Puncture the "eye" of the coconut with an ice pick and save the milk. Open the coconut by tapping along its length with a hammer. Remove the meat and peel away the brown skin.

Coarsely grate ½ of the coconut in a blender with the hot water. Blend again to liquefy. Pour through a sieve lined with two layers of cheesecloth, squeezing the cloth tightly to extract every bit of juice. Repeat the process with the other half of the coconut, using the same water.

Add the reserved coconut milk to the coconut. If the mixture does not yield 2 cups, add enough of the blender water to equal that amount.

Bring the coconut mixture to a boil and sprinkle with 2 tablespoons of concentrated agar-agar flakes. Cook at a constant low boil for 10 to 12 minutes, making sure that all agar-agar is dissolved. Stir honey into the hot coconut mixture. Add 2 cups of water and bring again to a low boil. Remove immediately from heat and stir in the vanilla and almond extracts.

Pour into a prepared 4-cup mold and refrigerate. To serve, unmold and top with pureed strawberries, raspberries, or the fruit of your choice.

Serves 4.

NOTE: Agar-agar will set before it has cooled so be sure to chill thoroughly.

The tiniest fairies live in minuscule nests neatly and elaborately woven to hang from tree limbs like the cocoons of butterflies. They look (if you can find them) like green, brown, or even flowered balls set deep within foliage. The fairies weave unobtrusive openings into the walls that become the doors and windows.

A tree fairy's home is kept warm by the yellow-green moss that grows thick and deep on the floor. A miniature table and chairs made from dried mushrooms and a milkweed-pod bed lined with dandelion down or milkweed-pod silk are the only furnishings needed to make a fairy's home complete. Some nests have two or three rooms, and occasionally there is more than one fairy in residence.

Eylie, a little green fairy who sometimes visits giants in their mountainous domain, loves to entertain at teatime. (As a matter of fact, teatime is a fairy invention, created simply as a reason for entertaining.) Sweets usually accompany the presentation of steaming herbal tea, which the fairies refer to vaguely as weed teas. Most popular for an afternoon tea is a cake made from fairy cheese. Since fairy cheese is very much like a humanly made soy product, tofu, this is a great recipe for those who love dairy products but may be allergic to them.

TEA CREAM CAKE

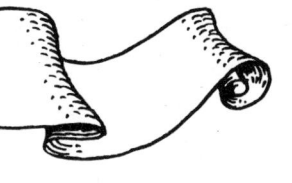

Crust
- 2 cups Grape-Nuts flakes, oat flakes, corn flakes, or granola
- ¼ cup ground almonds (optional)
- 1 teaspoon cinnamon
- 6 tablespoons oil or melted butter
- Filling (recipe follows)

Preheat oven to 350°.

Grind cereal in food processor or blender or crush with rolling pin between two pieces of waxed paper. Mix in cinnamon and melted butter. Toss all ingredients together with a fork until uniformly moistened. Press cereal mixture firmly into the bottom and along the sides of a 9- or 10-inch springform pan. Reserve two or three tablespoons for garnish.

Pour filling into the crust and garnish with extra cereal. Bake for 40 to 50 minutes. Remove from oven and cool thoroughly. Refrigerate. Serve plain or with fruit.

Filling
- 2 pounds tofu cut into 1-inch pieces
- ½ teaspoon salt or Vegesal
- ¼ cup lemon juice
- ½ cup sunflower oil
- ¼ cup honey and ⅓ cup maple syrup
- 1½ tablespoons arrowroot or cornstarch mixed with 2 tablespoons of water to make a paste
- ½ teaspoon vanilla

Using a processor or blender, cream all ingredients until smooth. Cream in two batches if using a blender. Filling can also be made using an electric mixer, but it will take a bit longer to achieve the smooth textures.

The little red fairies whose duty it is to meddle with the ill-tempered trolls must take care to stay out of sight, lest the trolls take them as pets. They are more of an aggravation than a help to the trolls, since they continually play pranks on their clumsy and unsuspecting charges. The capricious fairies will hide the trolls' fire sticks, causing great unrest and even fights, since one troll thinks nothing of accusing the others of stealing. After the melée, the fairies always return the "borrowed goods," secretly, of course. When they are discovered, the wronged troll is convinced that he has been the butt of a joke so the argument is continued.

Watching the ridiculous behavior of the trolls, though amusing, ultimately makes the fairies so contrite that they leave a peace offering of food at each dwelling. At first the wary trolls refused to eat the gifts left by the unseen troublemakers, but over the years they have learned to trust the offerings; however, the dull trolls still haven't made the connection between the offerings and the pranks.

Today the fairies left Honeynut Brittle, a fairy pièce de résistance. The trolls are afraid of bees, so they rarely get any honey to eat. The brittle is regarded as such a treat by the trolls that the fairies have come to use it only when they are feeling overwhelmingly guilty.

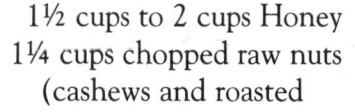

HONEY NUT BRITTLE

1½ cups to 2 cups Honey
1¼ cups chopped raw nuts (cashews and roasted peanuts are a particularly delicious combination)

Heat honey slowly until it reaches 295° on a candy thermometer (hard crack stage). Add the nuts to the honey and beat. Pour onto a buttered or oiled pan, let cool, and crack into pieces. Since honey tends to absorb moisture from the air, be sure to store in a tightly sealed container.

Although tupelo honey is most frequently used, you can experiment with other flavored honeys such as clover, wildflower, alfalfa, or orange blossom.

Fairies of all sizes are fond of drinks that sparkle and fizz. They generally consume fruit juices of all types, but the drink that is saved for special occasions is their lemon-ginger sparkle. Though they do not celebrate birthdays, as do the dwarfs, they do raise a glass to the first flower in spring, the colors of fall, a particularly beautiful cobweb, or the return of a prisoner from the frozen land of Daln. They celebrate the viewing of the northern lights, the coming of new fairies, and those who are more mischievious may even celebrate the success of a well-played prank.

CELEBRATION SPARKLE

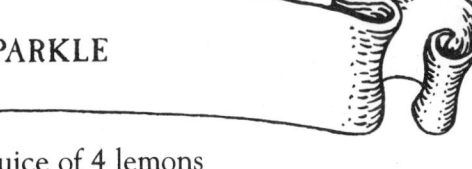

4 cups honey
2 gallons water
1 hand of ginger root, grated, or
1 tablespoon dried ground ginger
1 whole lemon
the juice of 4 lemons
¼ teaspoon yeast
¼ cup water
3 egg whites, beaten

In a large pot dissolve the honey in water over medium heat. Add ginger, beaten egg whites, and bring to a boil. Skim thoroughly and remove from heat. Strain through three layers of cheesecloth. Add whole lemon and set aside to cool.

When the mixture is lukewarm or 105°-110° on a thermometer, add the juice of four lemons and the yeast, which has been dissolved in ¼ cup of water. Stir well and let stand until cool.

Strain through cheesecloth and pour into bottles with new caps. Store in a

cool place for two days. Chill and serve.
Celebration Sparkle can be made as a handy concentrate by using only one gallon of water. Follow directions as above, but use no yeast. Store concentrate in refrigerator until ready to serve. Fill tumbler halfway with concentrate, add sparkling water, and stir.

Serves 24 humans and many fairies.

The language of the continent of Zir was developed by the fairies. Most of the inhabitants speak one or another dialect of it, except for the small community of Tiran humans. The fairies have tried time and time again to teach Zirimta to the humans, but the humans have always stubbornly refused to learn. With the use of the language comes a certain understanding about the true world of magic and a limited amount of power. This is the gift the fairies wanted to give the humans, but, sadly, only a few have accepted it.

The written Zirimtan word has an interesting and beautiful look. It is always scripted in red on handmade paper or cloth.

Here is a sample of the ingredients of a recipe written in Zirimta.

The fairies are among the oldest of Zir's inhabitants. Their magical power is great. Good fairies use their power gently; those who are mischievious use it adroitly and those who are corrupt use it horrendously.

Theirs is a society as complex as its diverse people, but it is founded on nature and thus has a natural balance. The balance that is Zir.

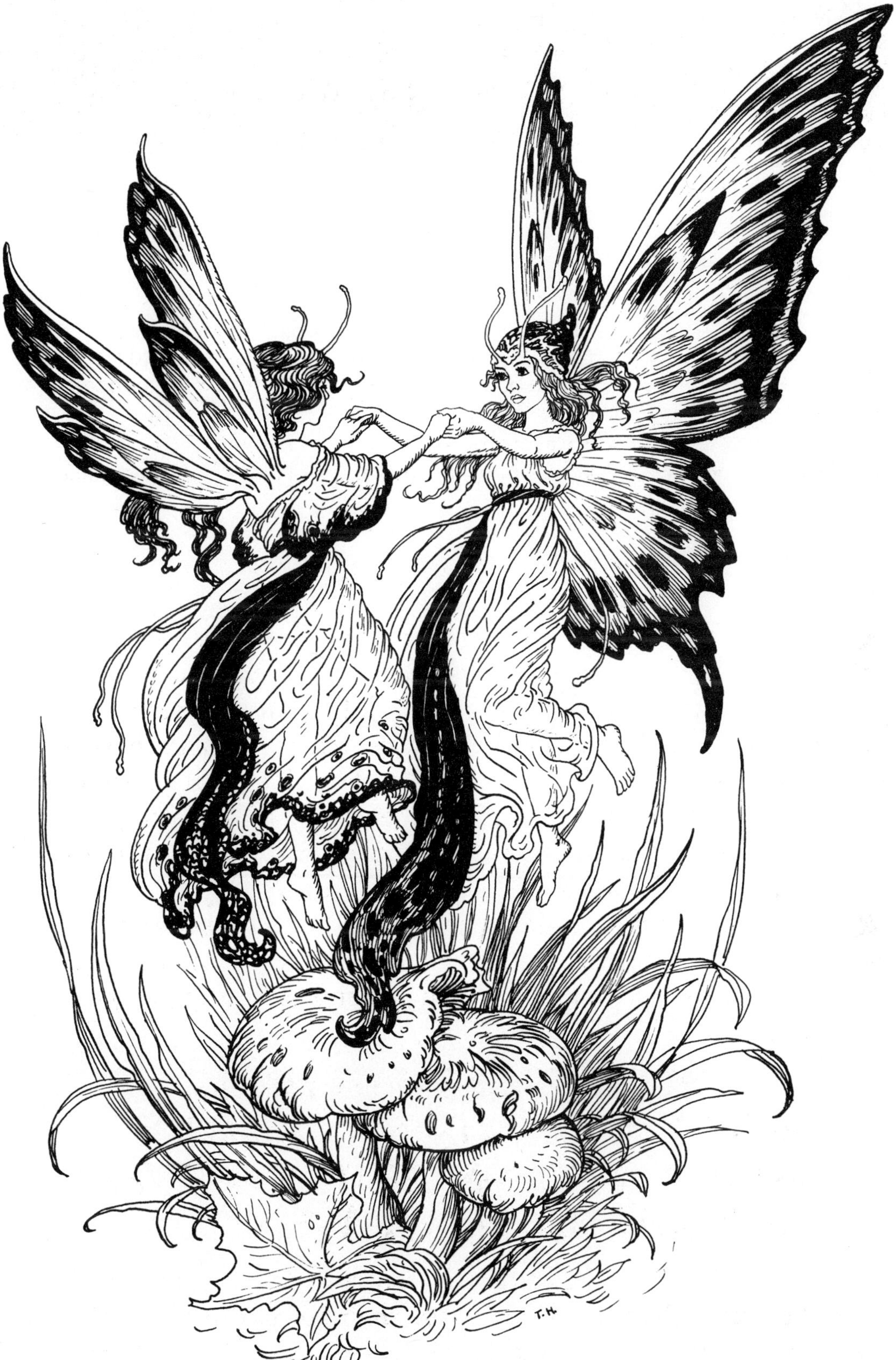
T.H.

THE MERPEOPLE

As ruler of the small land kingdom of Erii in the country of Mandria, King Dantri was possessed by the desire to find a real sorcerer or wizard who could perform true feats of magic. Each year, Dantri would circulate proclamations of intent, summoning all magicians to come and perform for him. Each was given a different task of wizardry to perform. The prize was half of Dantri's kingdom and his beautiful daughter for a bride. Many answered the call, but since none could prove his powers, all failed the tests.

One day a dashing blond man named Pembree arrived at the castle gate. He claimed limitless powers and the ability to grant any desire of the king. Dantri gleefully put him to the test.

Pembree was commanded to prove his ability by turning the king, his family, and the entire court into fishlike creatures and allowing them to romp in the depths of the sea for one hour. The blond stranger smiled. "Is that all?" he asked. "It is as good as done!" Pembree kept his word. But while the king and his court were frolicking in the sea, the duplicitous magician left them, returned to Erii, and laid claim to the whole kingdom.

The king and his sea people were left alone in their watery prison: their new bodies were well equipped for the strange environment, but all suffered a complete loss of memory about the way home. The courtiers were frightened and blamed King Dantri for their predicament. Bravely, the ruler took charge and led them out across the vast sea until they reached the welcoming shores of Zir. When the displaced creatures approached the beach they knew this would be their new home.

The Waterfall Lagoon became their surface court and the shoreline their fields for harvest. Deep under the ocean, in a grotto where the water is always calm, the merpeople built a spectacular castle where King Dantri resided in marine splendor, amassing all the wealth of the sea.

At first the merpeople had a great desire to return to the land, but as they learned the ways of the water and the richness and freedom of oceanic life, they readily accepted their fate. Upon King Dantri's first meeting with Alzar the wizard, he recounted his people's adventures. Alzar offered to remove the spell and return them all to human form. All refused but one. By this time they were somewhat skittish about wizards, but they had also grown satisfied with living their long lives free from the cares and ills of earth dwellers. In addition, they had attained magical powers of their own, which would be forfeited if the merpeople again became humans.

    The sea people live extremely long lives and can stay out of water for up to a week if kept damp. It is not unusual for a mermaid to pull herself out of the water and crawl along the shore to look for fruits, vegetables, or herbs. Mermen trade pearls or valuable pieces of sunken treasure for food or earthly trinkets.

These people love contact with other beings and make every effort to compel visitors to come to the seaside. Generous with gifts, they often grant wishes for their guests or present them with tokens of the sea's riches. The merpeople's terrible reputation for being the cause of shipwrecks or drownings has been passed down quite unfairly through human folklore. These acts are punishments for unprovoked acts of aggression against the ocean dwellers. Only the greedy who attempt to steal from the king's treasure or kidnap a mermaid for ransom must bear their swift and ruthless retribution.

The sea offers its inhabitants as many opportunities for earning their livelihood as the land does its people. The mermen grow sea vegetables and raise fish and crustaceans for food. The mermaids tend the sea cattle called cootles, which provide them with milk. The merpeople also hunt for game and treasure.

Merpeople eat a wide range of foods, including raw fish, sea vegetables, and even some poultry. When they are out in the open sea the ocean dwellers eat on-the-run meals consisting of whatever is available. However, when near shore they eat two meals a day—a light breakfast and an early-afternoon repast that is much heartier. On days when they have worked or played especially hard, they will snack in the evening, but that is not usual. Merpeople have substantial appetites, particularly mermen, who do the brunt of the work of catching fish and hunting treasure.

Breakfast is usually a fruit meal replete with fruit drinks, fresh fruit, and some type of cooked fruit dish. These crepes are the merchildren's favorite breakfast treat. They are also popular with the elf children who visit the lagoon.

COVE FRUIT CREPES

1¼ cup rice flour
⅛ teaspoon sea salt or kelp
4 eggs, beaten
1 teaspoon honey
1½ cup fruit nectar (apricot is very nice)
3 tablespoons melted butter
Grated nuts
Fruit filling (recipe follows)

Combine the honey, fruit nectar, and butter to the beaten eggs and mix well. Beat in the flour and the salt. Allow the batter to stand for 15 minutes.

Heat pan. Ladle a small amount of batter into pan (about ¼ cup) and tilt pan to coat thinly with batter. Cook until set and golden.

Spread crepes with about ½ cup of the fruit mixture each and roll up. Serve with Golden Sauce *(page 59)* and sprinkle with grated nuts. Allow 3 crepes per person, 6 crepes per merperson.

Recipe makes about 20 6-inch crepes.

Fruit Filling

10 large strawberries, sliced
2 bananas, sliced
½ ripe pineapple, cut in ¾-inch cubes
½ cup coconut, shredded fresh or desiccated

The merwomen generally do what cooking must be done. The mermen gather the groceries and clean the fish. Cooking is done on heated rocks or in open fires along the beach, but if the merwomen are near a hot natural spring they boil or steam the food. All meals are served in shells or on plant leaves. Coconut shells or bowls made of hollowed-out driftwood are often used. Foods are garnished with fresh flowers or herbs.

Although sea life can be very arduous, the merpeople, adults as well as children, play many water games. They always delight in playing with the happy dophins and porpoises. (The dolphins are not only wonderful playmates but exceptional bodyguards.) The sea people communicate perfectly with the dolphins. They can romp for hours, jumping high into the air to see who is best, turning somersaults, and twisting and turning under the sea's surface until the water churns. The merchildren and merwomen go for rides on the porpoises backs. After all the cavorting has completely exhausted the merpeople (the dolphins have much greater endurance), they laboriously swim to shore and drop on the beach. When sufficiently rested, they discover that they have developed enormous appetites. To curb it temporarily they snack on seaweed and crustaceans along the shore. But once they reach home, they swim deep into the sea to their ocean palace and polish off a dip or two while sitting on cushions of seaweed and moss.

This is a very easy recipe to make. The mermaids use fresh cheese made from their sea cattle, but humans can prepare this Sea Palace Snack with cream cheese.

SEA PALACE SNACK

1 bunch parsley
1 bunch scallions (use only the white part if a mild onion taste is desired)

8 ounces cream cheese
Pinch of kelp or sea salt

Clean parsley and scallions thoroughly. Place all ingredients in bowl of food processor or blender and process until smooth.

Merpeople use dried and toasted sea weed or sea vegetables to dip into their snack. Humans can substitute crackers or vegetables like celery sticks or cucumber slices.

Makes enough dip for 2 mermaids, one merman, or 6 humans.

The moon in all its phases holds special significance for these half-fish creatures. Even the scales on their tails have a unique property directly connected to the moon's light. On any moonlit night one can see the glowing greens and silvers of the faintly beaming mermaid's tail as she swims gracefully among the blades of kelp. Even after the mermaid has shed her scales, a process she undergoes three or four times during her life, the water sprites who live near the lagoon maintain their glow. By hanging the scales on trees the sprites make the grotto twinkle with a rainbow of lights when the sun slips close to the horizon.

The moon's full phase brings a special celebration for the merpeople. Full moon is the only time the merpeople have a late-night meal; it is a time for festivities, eating, singing, and storytelling. These people are extremely fond of hearing scary tales, and the children revel in the retelling of stories about the terrible humans and the great pink squid. But before all are tingling with fright, the merpeople enjoy a traditional full-moon dish. Visitors are asked to bring some of the necessary ingredients. The merpeople must have rice from the fairies and bacon and flour from the dwarfs before they can begin cooking Moonlight Shrimp.

MOONLIGHT SHRIMP

2 pounds large shrimp, shelled and deveined
2 tablespoons oil
1½ cups browns rice
1 cup chopped onion
1 cup V-8 or tomato juice
2½ cups water
3 teaspoons thyme
1½ teaspoons salt
8 slices bacon, cut in half
2 tablespoons butter
2 tablespoons flour
1 cup hot milk
1 cup grated sharp cheddar cheese or ½ cup Swiss and ½ cup Parmesan

Wrap each piece of cleaned shrimp with ½ slice of bacon and secure with a toothpick. Set aside.

In a skillet, brown the rice in the oil, then add the onion to the rice and sauté for one or 2 minutes. Pour in V-8 and water, and season with thyme and salt. Bring to a boil, then lower temperature to the lowest setting and cook, covered, for 45 to 55 minutes. (Do not lift lid until rice has cooked for 45 minutes.) When done, fluff the rice with a fork and keep warm.

While the rice is cooking, make a cheese sauce. Melt the butter in a sauce pan. Whisk in flour and let the mixture cook over low heat for two minutes. Pour in the hot milk, stirring constantly with a whisk until sauce is thick. Add the grated cheese and stir until it is melted. Keep finished sauce warm.

Broil shrimp 6 inches from heat, turning once.

To assemble dish, arrange shrimp on top of rice and pour cheese sauce over all. Serve at once.

Serves 2 mermaids, one merman, or 6 humans.

Although the merpeople have a monarchy, King Dantri rules in a very democratic manner. He presides, mainly, at swimming races, diving competitions, or moon festivals, but his most important duty is the coordination of all patrols that seek out sick or imperiled sea animals. The mermen diligently swim the Ziran shoreline, even venturing out into the vast ocean on these missions of mercy. Whales, dolphins, and sea otters will often accompany the search parties as escorts, especially if sharks or large squid are known to be in the area.

The mermen have rescued countless wounded animals,

carefully transporting them to the safety of the lagoon, where the mermaids nurse them back to health. Mermaids also care for orphaned baby sea mammals, teaching them the ways of the sea until they are able to look after themselves.

Seri, the King's daughter, has a nearly miraculous ability to heal any sick ocean creature, friend or foe.

She is also a great cook and can "heal" any hunger pains suffered by her charges or the mermen who return ravenous from their patrols. Still without a mate, she has many suitors. One of her most requested dishes is Kabobs Fruites de Mer.

Seri uses large fish bones as skewers for her kabobs. Lacking those, you can use the metal skewers preferred by most humans.

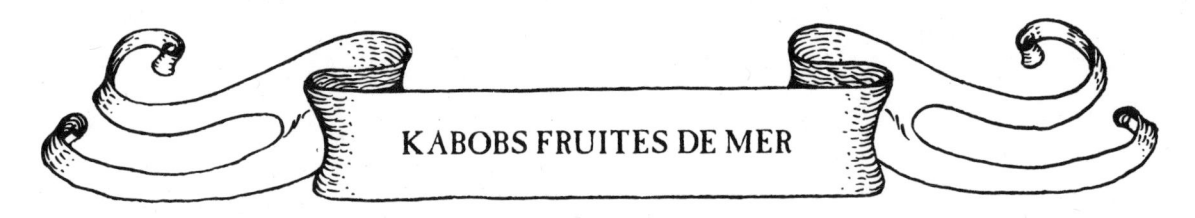

KABOBS FRUITES DE MER

½ pound medium shrimp
1 halibut steak, in 2-inch cubes
½ pound swordfish, in 2-inch cubes
½ pound sea scallops
1½ bell peppers, in 1-inch pieces
About 12 cherry tomatoes
8 ounces fresh mushrooms
1½ onions, quartered
Melted butter
Sauce (recipe follows)

Alternate shrimp, halibut, swordfish, and scallops on skewers with bell peppers, cherry tomatoes, and onions. Recipe will yield 6 to 8 kabobs.

Broil kabobs for 15 minutes under medium-high heat. Turn once during cooking and baste with melted butter.

Serve over wild rice or a mixture of brown and wild rice. Cover kabobs with sauce.

Serves 6 to 8 humans.

Kabob Sauce

For White Sauce:
4 tablespoons butter
4 tablespoons flour
1 cup milk
1 cup fresh stock or bottled clam juice
4 tablespoons white wine (sauterne)
¼ teaspoon chervil
2 tablespoons plus 1 teaspoon sherry
1½ tablespoons canned pimientos cut in ¼-inch pieces

4 to 5 tablespoons fresh mushrooms cut it ¼-inch dices
½ cup finely chopped onions
1 tablespoon capers, chopped
Pinch of freshly grated nutmeg
1 tablespoon and ½ teaspoon caper liquid
Scant ¼ teaspoon salt
½ teaspoon white pepper
5 tablespoons butter
2 or 3 tablespoons reduced fish stock

Melt 4 tablespoons butter over low heat in a saucepan. Blend 4 tablespoons flour into butter and cook, stirring constantly, for 3 to 5 minutes. Stir in slowly 1 cup of milk and 1 cup of fish stock or clam juice and cook, over medium heat, until thick and smooth.

Sauté onions in the butter, adding the mushrooms when the onions are just tender. Add wines, and stir in all remaining ingredients except for white sauce. Bring to a boil and simmer for three minutes and add to white sauce. Serve over Kabobs.

Agar-agar forms the basis for this lovely molded dish. It can be used as an entrée or salad. Mermaids serve Sea Mold in a conch shell with fresh sea kelp as a green accent. For humans, parsley or any leafy green vegetable will do very well.

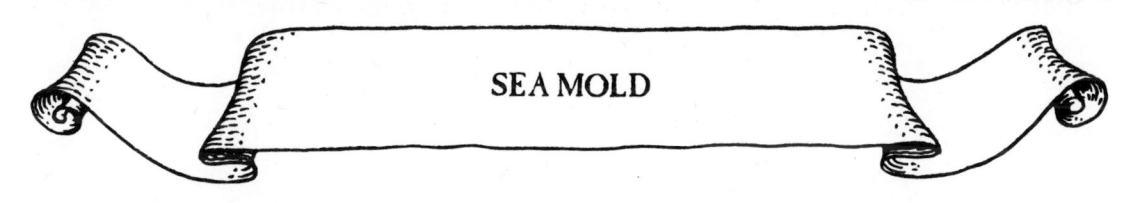

SEA MOLD

¼ teaspoon chili powder
1 4-inch piece kombu (kelp)
6 cups water
4 cups V-8 juice
⅓ cup chopped celery
2 cups peas, fresh or frozen
6 ounces langostino lobster (coarsely chopped), about ½ cup
8 ounces tiny shrimp, about 1 cup
10 tablespoons agar-agar

½ cup diced green pepper
⅔ cup scallions, chopped
1 bay leaf

Boil the kombu in a saucepan with 6 cups of water for 5 minutes. Strain, reserving the liquid. There should be about 4 cups.

Finely chop the kombu and set aside. Steam or boil lobster and shrimp and coarsely chop. Cut celery, green peppers, and scallions into ½-inch pieces. Steam peas only until they are bright green. (If using frozen peas, thaw completely but do not cook.)

Combine V-8 juice, 4 cups reserved kombu liquid, bay leaf, chili powder, and agar-agar in a large pot; bring to a boil and simmer 5 minutes. Strain through a sieve. Stir in vegetables, shell fish, and kombu, and pour into 8 large sea shells or an 8-cup mold. Refrigerate until thoroughly chilled. Delicious served with mayonnaise dressing.

Serves 16 to 20 humans or 8 to 10 merpeople.

Many of the mercy missions of the merpatrol take them into the cold oceans near Daln, the land of the ice fairies. The mermen approach this area with caution, for the evil fairies have been known to use their magic treacherously. Those of the merpatrols that have been lured onto the ice by the ice fairies' spells are doomed to do the ice fairy queen's bidding. These captives who are turned into ugly water gnomes or even uglier ice goons lash out at their own people, for the ice fairies need a vast army of slaves to seek not only material wealth but power over the peoples of Zir.

Some of these pathetic creatures have been rescued, and although Alzar the wizard is able to return them to their original form, their psychological recovery is slow. Since merpeople, like dolphins, are very sensitive to sound vibrations that echo through the sea, their best medicine is the happy sound of the merchildren at play. They are also soothed by the haunting tones of the conch horns played by the mermaids and the shell and bone harps plucked by mermen.

These ex-slaves are nursed by Seri, who feeds them herbs and many fresh fruits and vegetables. One of the foods served to help bring back the spirit of happiness to former captives is a merchildren's favorite.

Because the agar-agar sets in a matter of minutes, mermaids find this a great next-to-the-last-minute dish. It does have to chill, however, to taste its best.

ORANGE MER GEL

5 tablespoons agar-agar
4 cups orange juice
1 teaspoon orange rind
2 tablespoons honey
1 pint strawberries, sliced
Sections of 2 oranges

Bring agar-agar, orange juice, orange rind, and honey to boil and simmer 5 minutes. When mixture is slightly cool but not yet set, add fruit and pour into 6 ½-cup molds or a serving dish. Chill well and serve.

Serves 6 humans or 3 merpeople.

Off the western shore of Zir, just north of the Waterfall Lagoon, is the tiny invisible island of Itch-ka. There the old scribe, Meric, makes tablets from flattened sea shells upon which he chronicles the undersea civilization. The secret of this process was taught to him by the wizard Alzar. When the shells are flat, the scribe etches them with a sharp stylus and finally dyes them with an ink made from discarded insect skeletons. These inscribed shells are wrapped, neatly stacked, and eventually stored in a dry grotto on Zir.

Old Meric recounts the history and adventures of the merpeople, from their beginnings at Erii to the present. These shells also bear maps pinpointing the locations of all the king's treasure troves, information greedily sought by the pirates and Roona, the witch. Thus far, the evil ones' effort to find the grotto have been completely thwarted by Alzar and Aureena, whose powers guard the grotto's entrance.

    The old scribe is treated with great respect by all of the inhabitants of Zir. The mermaids spoil him terribly, waiting on him hand and fishtail while preparing his favorite dishes. Since one of his more frequently requested recipes involves the use of an oven, the mermaids constructed one by digging a pit and lining it with shells and rocks. Each time the mermaids prepare old Meric's favorite food, they build a fire in the pit and then remove the coals and ashes when they have burned down. By placing the foods to be baked in the pit and carefully covering it with hot stones the mermaids can successfully bake.

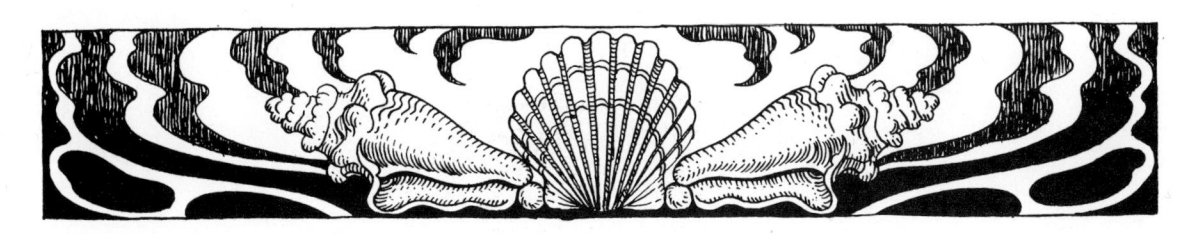

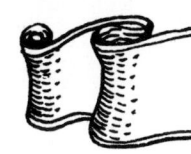

SCRIBE'S SPECIAL BAKED SHELLS

1 to 1½ cups Kabob Sauce (page 167)
½ cup cooked wild rice or brown rice
6 ounces canned crabmeat
¼ to ½ cup sautéd or canned mushrooms (optional)
Whole-wheat pastry dough (you can use mix)
Scallop shells

Preheat oven to 400°.

In a bowl, combine the Kabob Sauce, rice, and crabmeat. Add mushrooms if desired.

Spoon mixture into buttered scallop shells. Roll out pie dough and cut it to fit as a top crust over the filling. Seal well and crimp edges for a decorative look. Make slits for steam vents. Bake in a hot oven for 10 to 15 minutes or until crust is brown.

Serves 2 to 4 humans or one old merscribe.

Another of old Meric's favorites also requires the use of the mermaid's oven. It is delicious and very easy to make.

MERMAID PIT OVEN BREAD

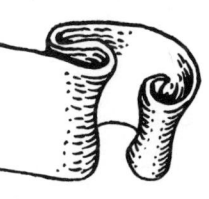

1 cup ground brown rice (use a blender or grain mill to grind)
⅓ cup unbleached flour or whole-wheat flour
½ teaspoon salt
2 teaspoons baking powder
1 tablespoon honey or turbinado sugar
1 cup milk
1 egg, beaten
3 tablespoons melted butter or oil

Preheat oven to 450°.

Combine all dry ingredients in a bowl. In another bowl, blend the milk, egg, and melted butter, then beat mixture into dry ingredients. Pour into 8-inch round buttered pan.

Bake for 20 to 25 minutes.

The merchildren try to imitate old Meric when they write their party invitations on shells. The most frequent recipients of shells are Neby, the wizard's dragon, and of course Alzar. Two or three times a year the dwarf or elf children are invited to come and play—their invitations are distributed by the waterfairies. When they can come, all of the children churn the sea with happy play.

For such a party the mermothers will plan a special large menu for the little ones, who inevitably work up terrific appetites. They will have:

SEAWEED ROLLS

RAW FISH CITRUS

SEA SPROUTS

SAVORY GRAINS

CONCH FRUITS WITH DRESSING

STEAMED SWEETS WITH TANGY DRIZZLE

COTTLE MILK AND SEAWEED JUICE

SEAWEED CANDY

To that basic menu will be added the many dishes brought by either the dwarfs or the elves, like those that follow.

Dwarfs find these rolls easy to take on a picnic. They can be served hot or cold.

DWARF'S MEAT ROLLS

3 pounds round steak (2 steaks) (dwarfs use any type of meat, especially venison)
¼ teaspoon salt
¼ teaspoon pepper
½ teaspoon paprika or more, to taste
1 tablespoon flour
1 large onion, chopped coarsely and sautéed
1½ cup sautéed mushrooms chopped coarsely
½ cup canned pimiento or fresh red pepper, chopped
¾ cup whole wheat-bread crumbs
1 egg beaten with ⅓ cup melted butter and 2 tablespoons stock
1 bottle of stuffed green olives, rinsed
⅛ cup butter or oil
1 cup Burgundy
½ cup beef or chicken stock

Preheat oven to 350°.

Mix salt, pepper, and paprika with the flour and rub over steaks. Pound steaks slightly to tenderize them.

Mix the onions, mushrooms, pepper, whole-wheat bread crumbs, and egg until consistently moistened and spread on the top side of the steaks. Arrange the stuffed olives in a lengthwise row across each piece of meat. Roll each steak jelly-roll style and tie with string. Brown rolls on all sides in a Dutch oven. Add wine and stock. Cover and bake for 1½ hours.

Serves 6 humans — or 3 dwarfs, as an appetizer.

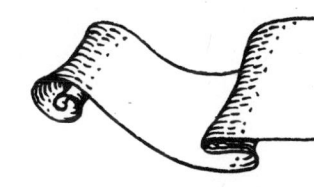

ELF FRUIT DIP

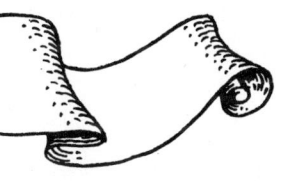

Version 1

1 cup sour cream
2 to 4 tablespoons honey
1 teaspoon ground cardamom
¼ teaspoon vanilla

Version 2

1 cup sour cream
3 to 4 tablespoons honey
2 teaspoons vanilla brandy (see Special Ingredients)

Mix ingredients together and serve either over strawberries or as a dip or topping for fruit. Very nice over fruit pies.

Merpeople eat seaweed of all types. Though they prefer it fresh, they will dry some for variation. They snack on dried seaweed just as humans snack on crackers. They have also developed many imaginative recipes for the delicacy; they wrap it around fish, sauté or broil it, or serve as is.

Here is one of the simple ways in which merpeople use Nori, a dried seaweed.

MERMAN'S SEAWEED SAUTÉ

1½ cups seaweed (nori)
2 carrots, julienned into strips 1½ inches long
2 onions, minced, or 2 teaspoons onion powder
2 tablespoons vegetable oil
2 teaspoons sesame oil
4 tablespoons tamari
1 large clove garlic, minced
1 1-inch piece fresh ginger root, minced

Cover nori with water and soak for at least ½ hour.

In a frying pan or wok, sauté the onions and carrot strips lightly in the oil. Add the ginger and garlic. Drain nori thoroughly and add to the onion-carrot mixture. Toss with the tamari, then steam, covered, for 4 minutes.

Serves 10 humans as a side dish, or 2 to 4 merpeople.

Courting is treated very casually by the undersea community, but when a mercouple decides that they will be mates, the union lasts until one of the partners dies. King Dantri presides over the pairing ceremony—a brief, no-frills affair held at the lagoon. Though the guests bring no gifts to the pairing, the two mermates offer special gifts to each other, a gesture that symbolizes the start of their life together. The merbride receives an armlet made of mother of pearl or metal, which she wears ever after on her left arm. The mergroom receives a belt from which hangs a small pouch containing a shell whistle.

In honor of the couple's pairing (the merpeople's word for "wedding"), a special dessert is prepared by the mothers of the bride and groom. A mildly alcoholic seaweed wine fermented for the occasion is used to prepare this dish, though humans can substitute sherry. Agar-agar was used to thicken the original recipe, but gelatin has been substituted here.

PAIRING-NIGHT PUDDING

½ cup turbinado sugar or ⅓ cup honey
1 cup heavy cream
1 envelope unflavored gelatin
1 drop natural red food coloring
¾ cup sherry
¼ cup white wine
Vanilla Cream (*recipe follows*)

Cook the cream, gelatin, and sugar or honey over low heat until sugar and gelatin are dissolved. Stir in the coloring. Add the wines and continue to cook, mixing thoroughly, for 1 minute. Pour into a greased 2½- or 3-cup mold. Refrigerate until firm. Serve with vanilla cream.

Serves 2 mermates or 4 humans.

VANILLA CREAM

½ cup light or heavy cream
1 egg yolk
3 to 4 drops vanilla extract

In a bowl beat the egg yolk with cream and vanilla until thoroughly blended. Pour over unmolded pudding.

Although pairing is not an elaborate event, the birth of a sea baby is celebrated with great festivities, perhaps because so few are born. The cause for celebration is even greater if the merchild happens to be born during the full moon, because merbabies born then are blessed with great healing powers or gifts of prophecy.

Invitations to join the merrymaking are always sent to Alzar the wizard, the Fairy Queen Aureena, the elf prince and princess, and the dwarf chieftains. Each bring gifts of toys, food, flowers, and ornaments to welcome the newborn.

The merpeople perform water dances to entertain their guests, and the mermen's feats of diving and swimming daring never fail to draw gasps from the audience. Each visitor receives a rare sea shell especially etched with names and dates by Meric as a keepsake of the occasion. King Dantri tells stories for the children until the sun sets; Alzar then begins his light show. Some visitors stay at the lagoon for a few days, if they have come from a great distance, but all of the guests want to prolong their visit.

One of the main sweets served at this festival is Sea-Birth Cake. Because its main ingredients come from the far corners of Zir, some are given as part of the birthday gift.

SEA-BIRTH CAKE

¼ cup oil
¾ cup butter, cut into very small pieces
⅔ cup chopped fresh apple
5 tablespoons grated orange rind (about 1 orange)
1 orange, chopped fine
2 cups raisins
1 cup currants
2½ cups fresh whole-wheat bread crumbs
⅔ cup whole-wheat flour
1 cup molasses
4 eggs, beaten
1½ cup chopped pecans
1 cup canned crushed pineapple, drained
2¼ teaspoons cinnamon
1¼ teaspoon ginger
¼ teaspoon nutmeg
½ teaspoon allspice
½ teaspoon cloves
1 teaspoon baking soda
4 tablespoons white wine
4 tablespoons rum, cognac, or brandy
Butter Sauce (recipe follows)

1 cup milk, scalded
¼ cup raspberry or other fruit jam

Combine the oil, butter, fruits, nuts, and jam in a large bowl. In another bowl, mix together the flour, salt, soda, and spices. Combine the butter-fruit and flour-spice mixtures well.

Beat the eggs until foamy, then blend in the milk and wines. Fold egg-wine mixture into flour-fruit mixture. Mix in the bread crumbs.

Pour into a well-greased, 3-quart, lidded steam mold or 2 one-pound coffee cans, filling no more than ⅔ full. Cover molds with lid or aluminum foil and place on a rack in a large pot. Add boiling water to reach halfway up the side of the mold.

Steam for 3 to 4 hours over gently boiling water, adding more water if necessary. Unmold and serve warm with Butter Sauce.

BUTTER SAUCE

¼ pound butter
1 cup brown sugar
1 tablespoon white wine
1 tablespoon vanilla brandy (see Special Ingredients)

Blend all ingredients well with electric mixer.

Dantri reigned in peace over his court at the Waterfall Lagoon until the day two ships dropped anchor just beyond the lagoon's mouth. From the deck of his ship, Captain Peg peered through his glass, until he spied a young mermaid sunning herself on the bank. She was draped in sea jewels. Her head was crowned with pink coral and her black hair was plaited with baroque pink pearls. Her wrists were circled with silvery disks. "I'm rich!" cried Captain Peg. "But how will I get the treasure from that half-fish?" He continued to watch, scheming. He would capture one of the maidens and force her to take him to the treasure. If she refused, Peg would hold her for ransom.

At dawn, a small, motley crew of evil-looking sea dogs headed by Captain Peg set out in a launch for the lagoon. As is the custom, the fish people welcomed the pirates with great hospitality. Each visitor was given a gift of a large pearl and a snack of tiny sweets. Captain Peg accepted the offering as graciously as a man of his ilk could, completely unaware that King Dantri knew exactly what he was plotting. After all, the good king had met many of Peg's type when he himself was a human.

After some conversation about the lagoon and what it was like being a merperson or a sailor, the talk drifted to the business of trading. By then the mermen had disappeared into the sea, leaving the old king and a few mermaids behind at the party. Suddenly the pirates snatched the king's daughter, Seri, and ran back to the launch. They had a difficult time with the struggling fish maiden, for she was very strong and much heavier than she appeared.

They had nearly reached the flagship when they saw their fellow crewmen jumping overboard. The ship was sinking. Just then, they heard the sound of snapping wood, and a large hole appeared in the launch's bow. The pirates had not time enough to shout — and they saw no one.

Seri got away, and the men swam to what remained of the

ship. A final warning was shouted out to them by the king.

> A pearl for a visitor to soothe his fatigue,
> But revenge on the pirates, who are filled with greed.

The sweets offered to the pirates or any special visitor who comes to court are Court Sweets and Mermaid's Munchies.

COURT SWEETS

8 ounces dried apricots, ground in food mill
½ cup honey
1 teaspoon cream
2½ cups desiccated coconut
⅔ cup finely chopped nuts

In a bowl, mix all the ingredients except nuts. Shape into balls and roll in nuts. Let stand two hours until firm, then chill.

Makes 4 dozen, enough for 3 merpeople.

MERMAID'S MUNCHIES

2 squares unsweetened chocolate, melted, or 6 tablespoons cocoa
⅓ cup honey
2 cups desiccated coconut
½ cup walnuts, finely chopped
1 teaspoon cream

Preheat oven to 350°.
Mix chocolate and honey over low heat until blended. Mix in other ingredients; if mixture appears dry and crumbly, add more honey or cream. Drop by teaspoons onto ungreased cookie sheet. Put in the oven and turn off heat. Leave for 15 minutes.

Makes 4 dozen, enough for 3 merpeople.

Cootles, the domesticated sea mammals kept by the merpeople, can grow to the size of a small whale. Their bulky bodies are covered with short, bristly, iridescent feathers that glow nearly as beautifully as the merpeople's tails when touched by moonlight. The placid cow-eyed creatures leisurely search out their meals in the lush kelp beds near the Waterfall Lagoon, but they have never yet refused to eat any vegetation gathered for them by the mermen.

The mermaids get milk from the cootles from which they make an array of dairy products. This rich milk has a very yellow cream, which the merchildren whip up to use on fruits and other sweets. A sweet pudding cooked by Talanta, a mergirl, uses sour cootle milk and pineapple. Here is how you can duplicate it using dairy products more accessible to humans.

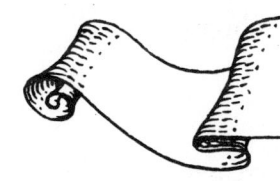

PINEAPPLE A LA COOTLE CREAM

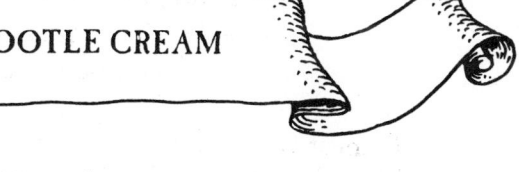

1 1-pound 4-ounce can crushed unsweetened pineapple and juice
3 tablespoons cornstarch
4 egg yolks
¾ cup honey
Pinch salt
1 cup sour cream

Drain the juice from the canned pineapple into a saucepan and reserve pineapple. Dissolve the cornstarch in the juice and add the honey and salt. Cook over medium-high heat until thick, stirring constantly.

Beat egg yolks slightly in a bowl. Add a small amount of the pineapple-cornstarch mixture to egg yolk and stir thoroughly. Blend the egg yolk into the thickened pineapple-cornstarch mixture, add pineapple, and cook for 2 minutes.

Remove from heat and cool. When cool, fold in sour cream. Can be served chilled or slightly warm.

Serves 4 humans, 2 merchildren, or one mermaid.

NOTE: ¼ cup dried or fresh coconut may be added. Merchildren also like to fold in ½ cup fresh wild strawberries when they can find them.

>We are the people of the sea,
>Humans we used to be,
>A sea of plenty we have found
>Only fools would leave for town

The words of King Dantri's silly song sums up the merpeople's feelings about their lives. They are unique and live in a special harmony with their environment. Though they do not hesitate to defend themselves against any who would do them harm, to friends and happy visitors the merpeople cannot be overly generous.

>I have the riches of the place
>And a mate with a pretty face
>What else could a fish man ask for
>Than to live happily ever after.

The land of Zir is a wonderful place, and to visit there through this book is to regain the happiness and imagination of childhood. Although this magic filled our lives for far too short a time, we wanted to share with you a small taste of Zir.

> You have seen a far-off land
> That is free from the erosions of man,
> A place and time that seem to be
> On the very verge of eternity.
>
> May your life be filled with fantasy,
> With the land of Zir as your key —
> A land of eternal imagination,
> A place of unending celebration.

SPECIAL INGREDIENTS

Many ingredients commonly used by the Zirans do not exist in our world, therefore, I had to find substitutions. Since my own cooking favors the use of natural foods over refined and processed foods, the substitutions I discovered while experimenting with ingredients are not only tasty but healthy.

Most of the ingredients used in this cookbook can be found on any supermarket shelf. Others can be purchased in specialty markets or health-food stores. Give them a try. These ingredients will not only add to the taste but also to the nutritional quality of the finished product.

AGAR-AGAR

This vegetable gelatin is derived from seaweed. It is stocked in most health-food stores in bar form or easy-to-use flakes. Originally discovered by merpeople, today it is commonly used in vegetarian cooking. Agar-agar sets into a nicer texture than does regular gelatin, which tends to get rubbery. It will gel at room temperature.

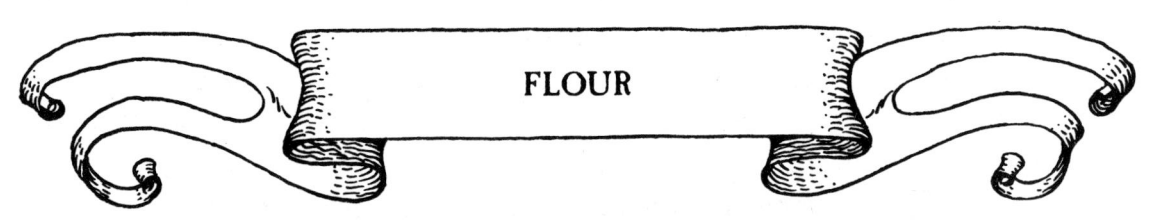

FLOUR

Some recipes in this book call for whole-wheat or a whole-wheat— unbleached white flour combination. You can use all unbleached flour, but there will be a decrease in nutritional value as well as a loss of the lovely nutty flavor and texture the whole grain offers. If for some reason you are unfamiliar with whole grains or if you wish to ease yourself or those for whom you cook into whole grains, I have developed a recipe for improving the nutritional value of white flour while altering the taste only minimally. To five pounds of white flour add

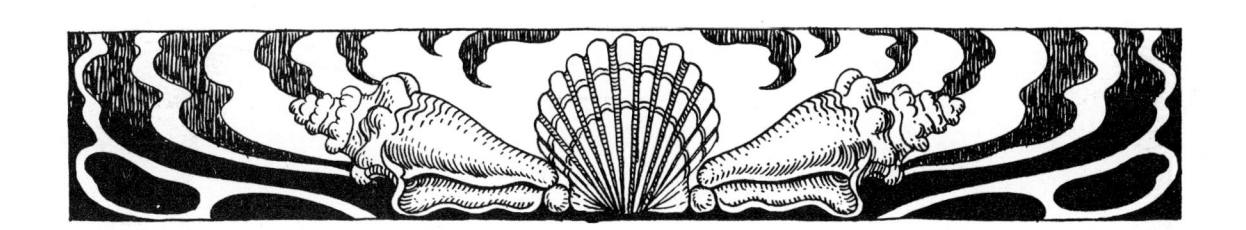

    1 cup bran
    ¾ cup wheat germ
    1 cup soy flour

As your taste starts to become familiar with whole grains start mixing in more whole-wheat flour. You will begin enjoying it so much that plain old white flour will seem tasteless.

Other flours and meals are used in the book. Try them. Interesting in flavor and texture, they include rice, potato starch, barley, corn, gluten, soy flour, rye and buckwheat. You can now purchase some at supermarkets, but others must be bought at health-food stores or specialty shops.

When measuring flour for use in the recipes in this book or in any other cookbook, you can eliminate sifting by stirring the flour vigorously with fork or wire whisk. This method can even be used in recipes in other cookbooks when instructions are given to sift dry ingredients together. All the great chefs may look on in horror but it does work and save time.

To substitute white flour for cake flour, fluff vigorously with fork or whisk, then measure. Remove 2 level tablespoons for each cup of flour needed in the recipe.

HONEY

Honey flavors are as varied as the flowers of the fields, and the type of honey you use can alter the taste of a recipe. Where honey is used as a sweetener in a recipe, I use tupelo honey unless otherwise specified.

Tupelo honey is considered by many to be the queen of honeys because of its mild flavor and its high percentage of fructose. This simple sugar is much more easily digested than the sucrose found in table sugar.

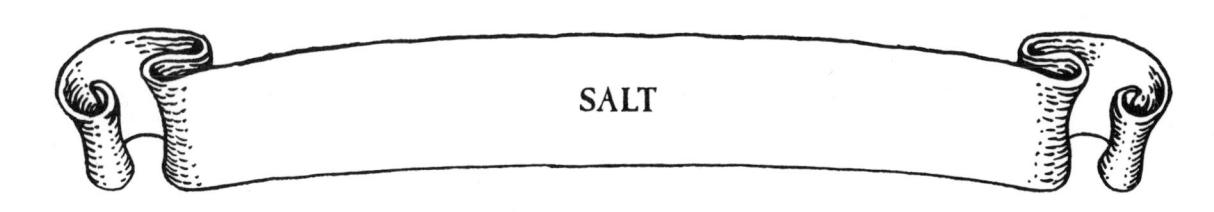

SALT

Salt is not used in most of the Ziran recipes, but because our human palate is so accustomed to its taste, I have included it. Try using sea salt; its taste is not different from table salt and it does contain a few minerals. Salt substitutes such as vegetable salt, Spike, Vegit or Vegesal given an interesting spark to food. One of the salty seasonings used by the merpeople is seaweed; kelp, dulse, nori and hijiki will all impart a salty flavor.

VANILLA BRANDY

A wonderful blend of flavors that enables you to make any dessert something special in no time.

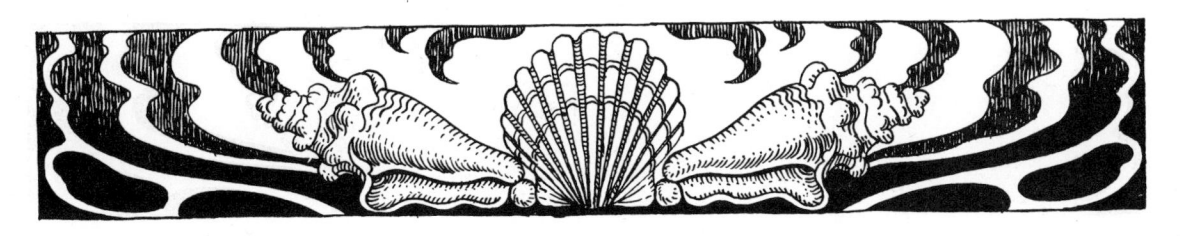

1 pint brandy   4 to 6 vanilla beans

In a blender, process brandy and beans until the vanilla is completely ground. Store in a bottle kept in a cool place for at least two weeks, allowing the vanilla to flavor the liquor. Keeps indefinitely.

INDEX

A

Agar-agar, 167, 183
  orange mer gel, 169
Almond loaf, queen's, 144–45
Alzar's party torte, 85–86
Amazon
  black cake, 59
  salad, 49
Appetizer(s)
  dip, 94
    elf fruit, 173
    Sea Palace snack, 163
    vegetable, 44
  rolls, 74–75
  spicy roll-ups, 73–74
Apple(s)
  baked, 25
  covered, 127–28
  crust, 129
  dragon, 25
  in fruit cobble, 20
  tarts, Autumn, 111
  turkey, stuffed, 7–8
Apricot(s)
  court sweets, 180
  fluff, 56
Artichokes, 103
Autumn tarts, 111

B

Bacon, in spicy roll-ups, 73–74
Baked apples, 25
Banana(s)
  pie, 77–78
  puff, 55
Barley-vegetable soup, 142
Beef
  dwarf meat rolls, 173

Beef (Continued)
  hearty, celebration, 124
  liver, in wedding stew, 123
  Petrie's stew, 125–26
  ribs à la dwarf, 8
Beet green(s), 18
Berry(ies)
  bread, 105
  drink, 117
  Tira's snow, 113–14
Beverages
  Amazon drink, 60
  berry drink, 117
  lemon-ginger sparkle, 154–56
  lion's tooth coffee, 26–27
  molasses mead, 28
  nog, spiced dwarf, 28
Bird in a coconut, 39–40
Bird in a crust, 70–71
Biscuit topping, 20
Black cake, Amazon, 59
Brandy, vanilla, 185
Breads, 11–15, 52–54
  cheese and crust, 75
  courting, 15
  flat, 132–33
  harvest, 14
  lump, 12–13
  mermaid pit oven, 171
  muffins
    à la Amazons, 54
    berry bread, 105
    moonlight, 98
    spiced, 73
  rolls
    à la Sizaeo, 53
    appetizer, 74–75
    bulgur, 107
    dwarf meat, 173
  round hearth cakes, 13
  rye, 11–12

Breads (Continued)
  rye (Continued)
    twists, 10–11
    whole-grain yeast, 10
  Brie cheese and crust, 75
Brittle, honeynut, 154
Broccoli
  Amazon salad, 49
  casserole, 48
  puff, 95–96
Brown rice, in mermaid pit oven bread, 171
Bulgur rolls, 107
Buns, curry, 71–72
  steamed, 51–52
Butter
  maple, 97
  sauce, 177, 178
Butternut squash, in triumph pie, 116–17

C

Cake(s)
  Amazon black, 59
  lemon-fennel, 81–82
  Neby's happy birthday, 87–88
    princess, 84
    sea-birth, 177–78
    tea cream, 153
    tree, 23
Calves' liver, in wedding stew, 123
Camembert cheese and crust, 75
Candy
  carob, 25–26
  court sweets, 180
  honeynut brittle, 154
  mermaid's munchies, 180
Carrot(s)
  -filbert ring à la unicorn, 45–46
  picnic, 101
  unicorn, 47
Casings, for sausage, 6
Casserole
  broccoli, 48
  vegetables in the oven, 100
  visitor's 68–69
Celebration sparkle, 155–56
Celery seeds, in seeded rye bread, 11
Cheese
  and crust, 75
  pie, 77
  puffs, special, 106
  Sea Palace snack, 163
Chicken
  bird in a crust, 70–71

Chicken (Continued)
  breasts, 39–40
  liver, 42
  and potatoes, 126–27
  sauced, 38
Chocolate, 180
Citrus
  surprise pie, 79–80
  tart, 109–110
Cobble, fruit, 20
Coconut
  bird in a, 39–40
  queen's molded, 151
Coffee, lion's tooth, 26–27
Corn, round hearth cakes, 13
Courting bread, 15
Court sweets, 180
Cous-cous, in grain patties, 101
Cove fruit crepes, 162
Covered apples, 127–28
Crabmeat, in scribe's special baked shell, 171
Cracked wheat, in bulgur rolls, 107
Crackers, oat, 94
Cranberries, in fruit cobble, 20
Cream
  in cheese pie, 77
  in most divine topping, 81
  sour, dip, 94
  vanilla, 114, 176
Crepes, cove fruit, 162
Crust
  apple, 129
  bird in a, 70–71
  cheese and, 75
  graham cracker, 78, 84
  for princess cake, 84
  for tea cream cake, 153
  Wilga's, 21
Curry, 43
  buns, 71–72
    steamed, 51–52
Custard, 19

D

Dandelion root, 26
  in lion's tooth coffee, 26–27
Dessert, 18, 19–29
  apples
    Autumn tarts, 111
    baked, 25
    covered, 127–28
    crust, 129
    dragon, 25

Dessert (Continued)
   apricot fluff, 56
   banana puff, 55
   biscuit topping, 20
   cakes
      Amazon black, 59
      lemon-fennel, 81–82
      Neby's happy birthday, 87–88
      princess, 84
      sea-birth, 177–78
      tea cream, 153
      tree, 23
   custard, dwarf's, 19
   fruit cobble, dwarf, 20
   fruit yummy, Reena's, 108–09
   mango mousse, 57
   pie
      banana, 77–78
      citrus surprise, 79–80
      fairy queen's, 115
      nut, 22–23
      triumph, 116–17
   pudding
      pairing night, 175–76
      pineapple à la cootle cream, 181–82
   tangerine shortcake, 58
   tart(s)
      Autumn, 111
      citrus, 109–10
      shells, 111
   Tira's snow, 113–14
   torte, Alzar's party, 85–86
   vanilla brandy for, 185
   Wilga's crust, 21
Dip, 94
   elf fruit, 173
   Sea Palace snack, 163
   vegetable, 44
Dragon
   apples, 25
   noodles à la, 66
Dressing
   herbal drizzle, 102
   salad
      à la peanut, for duck salad, 39
      lemon-honey drizzle, 143
      tahini, 144
Drinks. *See* Beverages
Duck
   à la oasis, 37
   salad, 38–39
   soup, 34
   wild drunken, 35–36

Dwarf(s)
   carob candy, 25–26
   custard, 19
   drumstick stew, 7
   eggnog, spiced, 28
   fruit cobble, 20
   greens, 18
   meat rolls, 173
   ribs à la, 8

E

Eggnog, spiced dwarf, 28
Eggplant souffle, 67–68
Elf fruit dip, 173

F

Fairy queen's pie, 115
Fennel, lemon-, cake, 81–82
Feta, in special cheese puffs, 106
Field salad, 143
Filbert(s)
   carrot-, ring à la unicorn, 45–46
   nut pie, 22–23
Filling
   for appetizer rolls, 74–75
   fruit, 162
   for Neby's happy birthday cake, 88
   for tea cream cake, 153
Fish, 5
Flat bread, 132–33
Flour, 185–86
Fluff, apricot, 56
Frosting, for Alzar's party torte, 86
Fruit(s)
   citrus surprise pie, 79–80
   cobble, 20
   crepes, 162
   dip, elf, 173
   filling, for cove fruit crepes, 162
   juice, 60
   Reena's fruit yummy, 108–09
   salad, 151

G

Game roast, 131–32
Gel, orange mer, 169
Gelatin, vegetable, 167, 183
Giblets, chicken, in bird in a crust, 70–71

Ginger, lemon-, sparkle, 155–56
Golden sauce, 59, 162
Goose, 35–36
Graham cracker crust, 78, 84
Grain patties, 101
Gravy, for wild drunken duck, 36
Greens, dwarf, 18
Ground beef, in Petrie's stew, 125–26
Ground lamb
  balls, 42
  wrong recipe, 70

H

Harvest bread, 14
Hazelnuts, in carrot-filbert ring
  à la unicorn, 45–46
Hearty beef celebration, 124
Herbal drizzle, 102
Honey, 183
  lemon-, drizzle, 143
Honeynut brittle, 154
Hors d'oeuvres
  cheese and crust, 75
  dip, 94
    elf fruit, 173
    Sea Palace snack, 163
    vegetable, 44
  rolls, 74–75
  spicy roll-ups, 73–74

I

Ice cream, vanilla, in fairy queen's pie, 115

J

Jebin's venison, 9–10
Juice, fruit, 60

K

Kabobs fruites de mer, 166
  sauce for, 167, 171
Kale, dwarf greens, 18
Kelp, in sea mold, 167–68

L

Lamb, ground
  balls, 42
  wrong recipe, 70
Leek, zucchini-, pie, 50
Leftovers
  sausage from, 5–6
  in stuffed apple turkey, 7–8
Lemon
  -fennel cake, 81–82
  -ginger sparkle, 155–56
  in golden sauce, 59, 162
  -honey drizzle, 143
Lion's tooth coffee, 26–27
Liver
  beef (or calves'), for wedding stew, 123
  chicken, 42
Lump bread, 12–13

M

Mamma Roca's sausage, 5–6
Mango mousse, 57
Maple butter, 97
Marinades
  for Jebin's venison, 9–10
  for tempeh and for tofu, 140
  for wild drunken duck, 36
Mead, molasses, 28
Meat rolls, dwarf, 173
Meringue, for banana puff, 55
Mermaid pit oven bread, 171
Mermaid's munchies, 180
Merman's seaweed sauté, 174
Milk
  in berry drink, 117
  nog, 28
Millet, in grain patties, 101
Mixed spices, 43
Molasses mead, 28
Mold, sea, 167–68
Moonlight muffins, 98
Moonlight mushrooms, 98
Moonlight shrimp, 165
Morning turnovers, 50–51
Most divine topping, 81
Mousse, mango, 57
Muffins
  à la Amazons, 54
  berry bread, 105
  moonlight, 98
  spiced, 73

Munchies, mermaid's, 180
Mushrooms
   moonlight, 98
   sauce, for tofu, 140–41
   in squash boats, 17

N

Neby's happy birthday cake, 87–88
Nogs, 28
Noodles, 34–35
   à la dragon, 66
   troll, 134
Nori, in merman's seaweed sauté, 174
Nut(s)
   honeynut brittle, 154
   pie, 22–23

O

Oat crackers, 94
Orange mer gel, 169

P

Pairing night pudding, 175–76
Pasta, spaghetti
   noodles à la dragon, 66
   troll noodles, 134
Pastry
   Alzar's party torte, 85–86
   bird in a crust, 70–71
   morning turnovers, 50–51
   See also Pie(s); Tart(s)
Patties, grain, 101
Peanut, salad dressing à la, 16
Peek pickles, 103
Petrie's stew, 125–26
Pickles, 103
Picnic Carrots, 101
Pie(s)
   banana, 77–78
   cheese, 77
   citrus surprise, 79–80
   crusts
      apple, 129
      cheese and, 75
      graham cracker, 78, 84
      for princess cake, 84
      for tea cream cake, 153
      Wilga's, 21

Pie(s) (Continued)
   fairy queen's, 115
   nut, 22–23
   triumph, 116–17
   zucchini-leek, 50
   See also Pastry; Tart(s)
Pineapple à la cootle cream, 181–82
Pork, in Mamma Roca's sausage, 5–6
Potatoes, chicken and, 126–27
Potter's cream soup, 4
Pretzels, rye twists, 10–11
Princess cake, 84
Pudding
   pairing night, 175–76
   pineapple à la cootle cream, 181–82
Puff(s)
   banana, 55
   broccoli, 95–96
   cheese, special, 106

Q

Queen, squash à la, 148–49
Queen's almond loaf, 144–45
Queen's molded coconut, 151

R

Raspberries, in most divine topping, 81
Reena's fruit yummy, 108–09
Ribs à la dwarf, 8
Rice
   brown, in mermaid pit oven bread, 171
   grain patties, 101
   for harvest bread, 14
Ricotta, in special cheese puffs, 106
Roasts
   duck, 35–37
      à la oasis, 37
      wild drunken, 35–36
   game, 131–32
   Jebin's venison, 9–10
Rolls
   à la Sizaeo, 53
   appetizer, 74–75
   bulgur, 107
   dwarfs meat, 173
Root, dandelion, 26
   in lion's tooth coffee, 26–27
Round hearth cakes, 13
Rye breads, 11–12
   twists, 10–11

S

Salad
　Amazon, 49
　duck, 38–39
　field, 143
　fruit, 151
　queen's molded coconut, 151
　Reena's fruit yummy, 108–09
　sea mold, 167–68
　soup from, 3
Salad dressing
　à la peanut, 16
　for duck salad, 39
　lemon-honey drizzle, 143
　tahini, 144
Salt, 184
Sauce
　butter, 177, 178
　for duck à la oasis, 37
　　on sauced chicken, 38
　golden, 59, 162
　kabobs, 167, 171
　for Neby's happy birthday cake, 88
　for Reena's fruit yummy, 109
　for tofu, 140–41
　tomato, for vegetables à la water fairies, 150
Sauced chicken, 38
Sausage
　casings for, 6
　Mamma Roca's, 5–6
Scribe's special baked shells, 171
Sea-birth cake, 177–78
Seafood
　kabob's fruites de mer, 166
　　sauce for, 167, 171
Sea mold, 167–68
Sea Palace snack, 163
Seaweed sauté, merman's, 174
Seeded rye bread, 11–12
Shells
　scribe's special baked, 171
　tart, 111
Shortcake, tangerine, 58
Shrimp, moonlight, 165
Snacks
　cheese and crust, 75
　Sea Palace, 163
Souffle
　broccoli puff, 95–96
　cheese puffs, special, 106
　eggplant, 67–68
Soup
　barley-vegetable, 142

Soup (Continued)
　duck, 34
　potter's cream, 4
　from salad, 3
　trail, 95
Sour cream dip, 94
Spaghetti
　noodles à la dragon, 66
　troll noodles, 134
Special cheese puffs, 106
Spiced dwarf nog, 28
Spiced muffins, 73
Spices, mixed, 43
Spicy roll-ups, 73–74
Spinach
　dwarf greens, 18
　salad, peanut dressing for, 16
Squash
　à la queen, 148–49
　boats, 17
　butternut in triumph pie, 116–17
Steamed curry buns, 51–52
Stews
　dwarf drumstick, 7
　hearty beef celebration, 124
　Petrie's 125–26
　wedding, 123
Stroganoff, vegetable, 146–47
Stuffed apple turkey, 7–8
Sugar-restricted diets, carob candy for, 25–26
Sweets, court, 180
　See also Candy; Dessert

T

Tahini salad dressing, 145
Tangerine shortcake, 58
Tart(s)
　Autumn, 111
　citrus, 109–10
　shells, 111
　See also Pastry; Pie(s)
Tea cream cake, 153
Tempeh, marinades for, 140
Tira's snow, 113–14
Tofu
　marinades for, 140
　sauce for, 140–41
Tomato sauce, for vegetables à la water fairies, 150
Topping
　biscuit, 20
　for citrus surprise pie, 80
　fruit dip, elf, 173

Topping (Continued)
    most divine, 81
Torte, Alzar's party, 85–86
Trail soup, 95
Tree cake, 23
Triumph pie, 116–17
Troll noodles, 134
Tupelo honey, 183
Turkey
    dwarf drumstick stew, 7
    stuffed apple, 7–8
Turnovers, morning, 50–51

U

Unicorn
    carrot-filbert ring à la, 45–46
    carrots, 47

V

Vanilla
    brandy, 185
    cream, 114, 176
    ice cream, in fairy queen's pie, 115
Vegetable(s), 16
    à la water fairies, 150
    casseroles
        vegetables in the oven, 100
        visitor's, 68–69
    dip, 44
    gelatin, 167, 183

Vegetable(s) (Continued)
    soup
        barley-vegetable, 142
        potter's cream, 4
        trail, 95
        stroganoff, 146–47
Venison, Jebin's, 9–10
Visitor's casserole, 68–69

W

Waffles, wizard, 96
Walnuts, in nut pie, 22–23
Wedding stew, 123
Wheat, cracked, in bulgur rolls, 107
Whole-grain yeast bread, 10
Wild drunken duck, 35–36
Wilga's crust, 21
Wine, in Jebin's venison, 9–10
Wizard waffles, 96
Wrong recipe, 70

Y

Yellow squash, 17

Z

Zucchini
    -leek pie, 50
    squash boats, 17